NIGEL REES

The Gift of the Gab

A Guide to Sparkling Chat

Macdonald

A Macdonald Book

First published in Great Britain in 1985
by Macdonald & Co (Publishers) Ltd
London & Sydney

British Library Cataloguing in Publication Data

Rees, Nigel
The gift of the gab.
I. title
828′.91409 PN6175

ISBN 0-356-10950-X

Photoset in North Wales by
Derek Doyle & Associates, Mold, Clwyd
Printed in Great Britain by
Redwood Burn Limited, Trowbridge, Wiltshire
Bound at the Dorstel Press

Macdonald & Co (Publishers) Ltd
Maxwell House
74 Worship Street
London EC2A 2EN
A BPCC Plc Company

Nigel Rees is much sought after for the sparkle of his chat. Terry Wogan, Michael Parkinson, David Frost and Johnny Carson are just five of the world-famous chat show hosts who have beseeched him to share a sofa with them. Runner-up at the Blarney International Festival (1973) and outright winner of the 1981 Wagga Wagga Palme d'Or, he has now written what will surely become the definitive guide to good talk in the modern age. Even more useful to the tongue-tied than *The Joy of Clichés*, *The Gift of the Gab* will delight and enchant with its many useful tips and – in places – exceedingly colourful language.

Contents

Introduction

Seldom can a book have had a more profound impact on popular behaviour than my earlier work *The Joy Of Clichés*.* Now, everywhere I turn, my ears are filled with the happy chatter of those fortunate people who have been guided by me in the correct use of clichés.

Nevertheless, it has to be said, *The Joy Of Clichés* dealt with a relatively specialist area of popular speech. It left virtually unanswered the vexed question of how the tongue-tied can overcome their diffidence and start to make sparkling conversation in private or hold forth, boldly, in public.

Take note of the following sad cases:

1) Bernard L. (this is not his real name). Bernard is forty-seven and chairman of a large computer company. He is well on the way to becoming a millionaire, receiving a knighthood and buying a football club. But he is not what you would call socially 'ept'. He can handle the 'big talk' all right (he would hardly have got where he is today without it); it is the small talk he is absolutely hopeless at.

2) Germaine G. (this is not her real name). Germaine is twenty-one, has a small dimple and works as a vet's receptionist. Not so long ago she wrote to Unity Hall, the agony aunt of the *News of the World* (9 December 1984), with this complaint:

> 'When I'm in company, I don't talk to anybody because I can never think of anything to say. I have a

[1] (Macdonald, 1984; Futura, 1985).

boyfriend who's in prison. When I go visiting with his family, they chatter on happily, but I sit there silent. My lad's always saying, "Talk to me." But I get embarrassed as I am afraid of being boring if I speak. What do people talk about? Please help, because I don't want to lose my boyfriend. How can I make conversation?'

3) Russell H. (this *is* his real name). Russell H. is a TV chat show host and confirmed bachelor. He perspires slightly under the lights. Driven to desperation, he answered a newspaper advertisement headlined:

'ARE YOU A BORE?

'A world-famous educationalist reports that there is a simple technique that makes you an interesting person in a matter of days ... To acquaint all readers of the *Guardian* with the easy-to-follow rules, the educationalist has printed full details of this interesting self-training method in a 24-page book ...'

Alas, although Russell enrolled on an expensive twenty-six week course, *no one noticed the slightest improvement in his conversational powers* ...

Wondering how I might be of assistance to such wretched people, I chanced upon an advertisement in the *Radio Times*:

'KISS THE STONE ... And get the Gift of the Gab ...
The Most Interesting People Go To Ireland.'

I immediately left for Cork and motored the short distance to Blarney Castle. Climbing to the top, I inquired of a youth about the procedure for kissing the Blarney Stone – famed in song and story for bestowing the gift of tongues to those who touch it with their lips. He gestured to a break in the battlements from which a capacious and rather elderly female bottom was protruding. Several hapless Irish peasants had apparently been attempting to lower the American tourist (to whom this bottom belonged) halfway down the castle walls so that she could buss the somewhat inaccessible brick. They were now wrestling to get her back up again.

Undeterred by this appalling spectacle, the next victim, a bison-like Texan, was also lowered over the edge. I watched with mounting horror as he disappeared from sight. At last, I could stand it no longer, left immediately and returned to London. To this day I have no idea whether the Texan was ever returned to the relative safety of the castle roof – or whether he plunged headlong, beyond the stone, in futile pursuit of his spectacles, false teeth, credit cards and lunch.

Clearly, kissing the Blarney Stone was not a route to conversational ease that I could safely recommend to anybody.

What were the alternatives? Well, let me pass on Unity Hall's advice to poor Germaine G. I quote:

> 'Save up tit-bits of things that have happened to tell your boyfriend. Read the newspaper and have an opinion on what's going on. Watch TV and talk about your favourite programmes. Most important – ask lots of questions. This makes other people do the talking for you while they answer.'

At least this is more dignified than being dangled over the edge of Blarney Castle, but I have a feeling that our Unity is passing the buck here. Asking questions is all very well, but it is no substitute for real conversation.

Then it came to me: what was needed was a manual of conversational jewels of the type once compiled, albeit in Ireland, by the celebrated Dr Jonathan Swift. His *Complete Collection of Genteel and Ingenious Conversation According to the Most Polite Mode and Method Used at Court, and in the Best Companies of England* comprised over a thousand witty sallies. For example:

> NEVEROUT: 'Well, miss …'
> MISS NOTABLE: 'Ay, ay; many a one says well, that thinks ill.'
> NEVEROUT: 'Well, miss; I'll think of this.'
> MISS NOTABLE: 'That's rhyme, if you take it in time.'
> NEVEROUT: 'What! I see you are a poet.'
> MISS NOTABLE: 'Yes; if I had but the wit to show it.'
> *(A puff of smoke comes down the chimney.)*
> LADY ANSWERALL: 'Lord, madam, does your ladyship's chimney smoke?'
> COLONEL: 'No, madam; but they say, smoke always

pursues the fair, and your ladyship sat nearest.'

LADY SMART: 'Madam, do you love bohea tea?'

LADY ANSWERALL: 'Why, madam, I must confess I do love it; but it does not love me ...'

The good doctor first published his helpful advice, however, as long ago as 1738. Think what that means. For very nearly two hundred and fifty years there has been no comparable guide to polite conversation. No wonder Bernard L., Germaine G. and Russell H. have been finding their small talk so difficult.

I resolved, there and then, to fill the gap with an (obviously much-needed) up-to-date manual of my own, even if, in keeping with the modern age, some of the material I gathered had to be slightly less polite than Dr Swift ever envisaged. *The Gift Of The Gab* is, if you like, my own present of verbal power to those less fortunate in these matters.

It may bc the case that doubters will declare that good talk cannot be taught and that it must occur spontaneously or not at all.

I cannot agree with this view. It seems to me that the essence of good conversation springs from the speaker's knowing how to say the right thing at the right time. This is a technique that, quite clearly, can be acquired in advance. It is no secret that some of the noted conversationalists of history, to mention merely some of the more obvious examples, Oscar Wilde, Mme de Sévigné and William the Silent, actually practised their *bon mots* in private beforehand. When they struck conversational gold, it is common knowledge that they often repeated their best lines many, many times thereafter.

In addition, there are certain approaches to the art of conversation which cannot be expected to arise naturally and must therefore be taught. I remember once discussing the whole subject with that brilliant animal-trainer and spirited conversationalist, Mrs Barbara Woodhouse. She remarked how she had been taught, as a girl, that it was the responsibility of each participant in a conversation to keep it flowing, bouncing the ball back and forth, so to speak, and not hogging it. Quite how Mrs Woodhouse's celebrated technique of blowing up the nostrils of those she instructs could be applied to conversation practice, alas, I never got round to asking her, as getting a word in edgeways was rather a problem on that occasion.

Another acquaintance who is never stuck for a word, Sir Roland Butter, the QC and closet hand-jiver, is a keen propounder of the idea of 'conversational etiquette'. By this he means that it is not sufficient to have a ready-made battery of witty ripostes, dry thrusts, and amusing sallies up one's sleeve: it is equally important to know precisely when and where it is appropriate to trot them out. I am most grateful to Sir Roland for his guidance on this topic. How many times have I presented a query to him with the words, 'But does one really say that in the best circles?' only for him to reply: 'Yes, of course one does, dear boy. One has been in the best circles and *one knows*!'

Then there is the question of how to get a conversation going after a long silence. I have horrific memories of my youth when, surrounded by relatives, a great hush would suddenly fall upon the assembled company. For hours on end nothing would pierce the conversational doldrums but the steady ticking of the grandfather clock, the mournful hiss of the gas fire, and the distant moan of a neighbour's Hoover. If only I had known then, and been able to put into practice, the verbal combustion technique known as the Auntie Addie 'Poison' Remark (named after a less reticent relative with a noted way with words.)

To her and to my other advisers, past and present, I am more grateful than I have words to express, though I am sure they will supply me with them in due course.

It was Pascal, I think, who said, 'The conversation is the man'. How true – and to think that he, like Swift, never had the opportunity of appearing on a television chat show ... One only has to think of the unfortunate story related to me by my good friend, Mr David Frost (rather more prone to asking questions than answering them, but a good fellow nevertheless), concerning his lengthy intercourse on the television with ex-President Richard M. Nixon.

During a break in recording the historic interviews, Mr Nixon clearly felt obliged to make some sort of small talk with David and asked, somewhat woodenly, 'Did you do any fornicating this weekend?'

Could there be a more appalling example of bad talk? (I must remember to send a copy of this manual to San Clemente, or wherever he skulks nowadays. It is never too late to learn.)

So, whoever it is you are talking to and whatever the circumstances, I am sure you will find appropriate advice in *The Gift Of The Gab*. Bursting with freshness and vitality, it is a Golden Treasury of choice idioms and choice expressions. If you are ever at a loss for words, it will fill any gap in the conversation; if you are ever humming and hawing, it will soon have you talking nineteen to the dozen. It will give you a command of language, enable you to say your piece, and render donkeys incapable of elegant motion. With *The Gift Of The Gab* by your side, your silver tongue will be loosened, your words will spin, and should the conversation ever flag, you will instantly be able to revive it.

Part 1
What People Should Say

Airline Pilots

British airline pilots fall broadly into two categories. (You'll find a lot of that in this book, incidentally. I mean, there are broadly two categories of most types of people – those who fall into two categories and those who don't. But still ...) There are pilots with ex-Battle of Britain voices who welcome you aboard after you have been stuck in some malaria-infested foreign part and make you feel that there's nothing that a nice little G-and-T won't put right. Or, less satisfactorily, there are chaps with slightly 'off' accents. Very good at their jobs, you understand, but probably living lives of quiet desperation with a Volvo and a minor drink problem a few miles outside Dorking.

And, as for *foreign* airlines, well, one knows that English is the international flying language but, honestly, most of their pilots are not up to it. I was on a Thai International flight once, all very chummy, accommodating stewardesses, free orchids and so on, but the pilot, well, frankly, he couldn't string two words together without a twenty second pause between them. One wondered how he would have coped if our plane had been roaring towards another at a closing speed of several thousand mph. Would he have been able to get out 'Stop!' or 'I say old chap!' in time to save us? I rather doubt it.

No, when we are dealing with the language of pilots, there is only one lot to pay attention to: those who fly with American airlines. What a fine breed of men. Nevertheless, I don't think I have ever actually seen one on a plane. I've seen them striding through departure lounges, of course, looking like the more distinguished type of soap opera actor. In fact, I suspect that is what they are. No, very rarely have I seen one aloft. Hence, frequent travellers on

American airlines, such as myself, are forced to wonder, solely on the basis of what comes over the intercom:

1) Whether the pilot is always one and the same – i.e. there is only one American pilot and he is present on every single flight. I don't know how he manages it, but I am led to this conclusion by virtue of the fact he always has the same voice.

2) As this scenario seems a bit unlikely, I have to ask myself whether the pilot ever actually says a word (assuming there is a pilot and the flying is not all done automatically). Instead, I suggest, his words are all pre-recorded.

3) And if this is equally unlikely then perhaps there are lots of different American airline pilots but, before they take charge of the controls, they all go to a special school where their voices are trained to conform to the husky, butch, laconic mode.

Working on the assumption that 3) is the right answer, I strongly suspect that American airline pilots are probably all trained to say the following types of thing:

'Er ... good evening, ladies and gentlemen, this is your captain – Captain Nixon – speaking. I'd like to welcome you aboard this wide-bodied Sooper Dooper Boeing 747 for the direct service, New York to London. **I must apologize for the very slight delay** of five hours you've had in the departure lounge. **I'm really very terribly upset about this. Believe me**. Now, I have to tell you, I'm sorry but we don't expect to be getting aloft for a very long time yet. We have to wait for clearance from Kennedy control. **At the outside I don't expect this to be more than** seven **minutes**. Meanwhile I hope you enjoy the flight, and once you're asleep I'll be waking you up with some interesting but [*inaudible*] facts about the points of interest we are passing over.'

Rather a one-sided conversation, I agree, but a brilliant piece of chat. The whole point of this Welcome Aboard speech is to make the passenger fully aware who is in charge. The pilot casually refers to a delay of five hours as a 'very slight' one. In the same breath, he is apologizing deeply for a terrible delay which may only amount to seven minutes. The passenger is made to think that *he doesn't know what to think*. Or that all he can possibly do in the circumstances is to begin to wait for the inedible food that the air stewardesses will be bringing him some day. And shut up. But he must sense that Captain Nixon has everything under control. The passenger must feel that, although he is in a tubular cattle truck whizzing across the Atlantic at 550mph, Captain Nixon is on a par with the likes of Christopher Columbus or Neil Armstrong when it comes to getting this kind of show on the road. (Incidentally, at the height of Watergate I was on a TWA flight that *was* in the charge of a Captain Nixon. Quite a lot of nervous thigh-slapping went on, I can tell you.)

In no time at all (if you are flying New York to London), you have had your dinner and watched the in-flight movie. The lights are turned down and, hey presto, five minutes later, dawn is coming up and you are being served with breakfast (or what airlines think of as breakfast – which is like any other meal but with a portion of grapefruit.) It is at this point that the pilot comes on with one of his best lines:

> 'Er ... ladies and gentlemen, I hope you have had a refreshing night's sleep. **We will shortly be approaching the London area ...**'

This is also designed to assert his superiority and make the passenger wonder whether or not the pilot knows there are *two*, if not three, airports in 'the London area'. The passenger thought he was going to Heathrow; the pilot is now dangling the possibility of a jettisoning at Gatwick – or, heaven forbid, Stanstead.

Should you find yourself stacked above any, or none, of these airports, the pilot will pull out all the laconic stops in an effort to 'keep you informed':

> **'I've just heard from planet earth'**

he will say, 'that, whatever.' This is supposed to be a hoot.

I would put it on a par with what I heard once on a flight from Miami to New Orleans. It was an unusual flight (Eastern Airlines, I think) in that the plane was almost completely empty and just as we were coming in to land, a couple of hundred feet from the runway at New Orleans, we shot right up into the air again. Pause. The pilot came on and said, drily:

'Well, folks, I think we'll try that one more time ...'

The thing is that up to the moment we nearly crashed the *pilot hadn't uttered a word.* Not a mention of 'planet earth' or the 'New Orleans area' or anything. It was very unsettling. I mean, it was more unsettling than if he *had* said these things. Pilots should.

Astrologers

I am using this term to encompass fortune-tellers, psychics, palmists, clairvoyants and tea-leaf analysts as well. The first such person I consulted about my future was a certain Gypsy Smith, a female palmist with a magic ball, on the promenade at Blackpool in 1968. She told me I had a long life-line, which was nice. That I would have three children (I haven't). That I would be financially better off after marriage than before (possibly). That at the time I had an older woman and a younger woman interested in me (I couldn't think who the older woman was). That I would get an opportunity to go abroad (which I should not accept if I wasn't keen). All this cost me 10/6.

But Gypsy Smith did reveal what all fortune-tellers should tell their clients:

'There is a big change coming in your life.'

That is the really important part.

More recently I had my astrological chart done for me by the immensely famous Mr Russell Grant ('The Queen Mother's Astrologer') who is also noted for his psychic turns. This was on a television programme in the course of which Mr Grant described me as 'eccentric' – a likely story – and utterly failed to predict that I would win the Eurovision Song Contest, as he had previously done for Buck's Fizz (see GUESTING ON CHAT SHOWS.)

Fortunately, Mr Grant later gave me a private sitting – not that there was very much room for me after he'd sat down – and a much more reasoned exposition.

Subsequently, I have paid very close attention to the sorts of things astrologers should say. At the risk of revealing closely-guarded trade secrets, I am publishing the following vital examples to help aspiring astrologers to say the right thing:

'You will receive something interesting through the post ...' (they should predict this in the latter half of December)

'You will get an opportunity for travel ...' (they should predict this in August)

'I think there'll be an earthquake' (they should predict this for the year ahead)

'There will be changes in the Kremlin' (ditto)

'Everything is either going to get worse or get better ...' (if writing this in a magazine it is important that nothing gets better until the end of the month ... when the next issue is published.)

Australian Airline Booking Clerks

Australian airline booking clerks must hold themselves in readiness for the day when they are dealing with the archetypal vulgar Australian male known as an 'ocker' or 'okker'. Should the fellow want to fly, say, to Alice Springs on a Fokker Friendship aircraft and the plane happens to be full, they should inform him so, using the immortal words:

'Sorry, okker, the Fokker's chokka.'

Bank Managers

There is a theory that people choose their jobs according to what they fear. I am a writer: therefore I must be frightened of words and do the job in order to come to terms with them. A bit potty, I agree but, when it comes to bank managers, there is evident truth in the theory. Bank managers are quite clearly frightened out of their skulls at the thought of handling money.

You grovel your way into the office of one of the breed to try and raise a loan and there he is cowering in a cupboard and shouting:

'For God's sake, don't ask me for any money! I don't know what it is! I've never heard of it! Horrible, green, crinkly stuff . . .!'

Should this approach not put you off, the bank manager will be forced to pretend that a loan is very difficult to get, impossibly expensive to maintain and, not to put too fine a point on it, not the sort of thing his bank ever has anything to do with.

At this stage, if you tell him you are a writer or a broadcaster or almost anything other than a bank manager, he will declare:

'Oh, you're in that rat race, are you?'

You have to admit, from his point of view, it can be very effective.

Bank managers should practise these invaluable lines.

Booksellers

A strange race, booksellers. Rather like hoteliers (*q.v.*), I always think. In their previous careers they have usually worked for large organizations or been in the services and they now want to start a job which has as little as possible to do with other stupid human beings. So they open up bookshops in out of the way places. And the really awfully annoying thing is that people *will* keep bothering them still, *really* stupid people who don't know the title of the book they want, let alone the name of the author, and certainly not that of the publisher.

So booksellers have to be protected. They must always say:

BOOKSELLER: 'Sorry, **we're out of stock at the moment.'**

CUSTOMER: 'Could you get it for me?'

BOOKSELLER: (*sharp intake of breath*) 'Well, it would

take several months. Publishers are so unreliable these days. They never send their reps round here, you know ...'

CUSTOMER: 'I just thought you might have had it. I thought it was the No 1 Bestseller?'

BOOKSELLER: 'Ah, maybe so, but **there's no demand for that sort of thing in this area**, I can tell you.'

CUSTOMER: 'Oh, I rather enjoyed his first one.'

BOOKSELLER: 'His *first* one, maybe. But **his last one didn't do very well for us.'**

CUSTOMER: 'Well, perhaps I won't bother then ...'

BOOKSELLER: 'That's right ... that's right! Go back to your bleeding home computer and your bleeding television – but don't blame me if the printed word has perished by the turn of the century ... Strewth! Customers! Publishers! Idiots!'

Traditionally, the foregoing is best rendered in the simple statement:

'Lots of people have asked me for that – but we don't stock it because there isn't any demand.'

Bores

Strange as it may seem, I am pretty sure that most boring people know that they are. Boring, I mean. So it is most impolite of non-boring people to say to them:

'Put another record on!'

because, in fact, bores are either secretly proud of being boring or incapable of doing anything about it. That is the reason why they inevitably conclude their recitations with:

'And that, my dears, is how I came to marry your grandfather ...'

and ask:

'I'm not boring you, am I?'

which, in most cases, goes some way to disarming agreement.

If you think you fall into the boring category then I suggest you bear the following phrases in mind should you ever go along to record an interview for the radio. Ignore the nervous expressions of, 'That was wonderful ... *really*', from the production staff and assert:

'That wasn't very good, was it? Can we do it again?'

Should that fail, use:

'Can I hear it played back?'

If they still insist it was wonderful, really, you will have to resort to the very effective:

'Can I stay behind and watch it being edited?'

But I hardly need tell you this. Boring people invariably ask these questions. Go to it.

Business Executives

I can speak with some authority on this subject, as for many years I had 'Business Executive' in my passport (well, it sounded less naff than 'Company Director', although it can mean as much or as little.)

My first passport, just to digress, had 'Student' in it. Then I put 'Broadcaster', until the Soviets refused me a visa in 1968. That was when I became a 'Business Executive' and began agonizing over what I would put in the next time I had to renew my passport. I felt that 'Author' sounded a bit pompous, and might lead to further trouble with the Russians. I eventually settled on 'Word Processor' (which seemed to sum me up), only to discover that you no longer had to put your profession in your passport.

(But, as I say, I digress.)

Business Executives should opt for the phrases, without exception, that express their inner dynamism and purpose. They should mix a few of the following together:

'We must consider the political, optical, visual aspects of the situation ...'

'We must probe the grey areas for a concrete solution ...'

'We must have hands-on involvement in an arm's length situation ...'

'We must invest in instalments – i.e. we need two bites at

the cherry and to spread the jam on a rolling programme ...'

'We must get both feet under the door and take a long-term view ...'

(I am very grateful to Mr Christopher Boddington for his careful tuition in this section.)

Other useful phrases include:

'When the rubber hits the road, cost comes walking in on two feet.'

'Let's hit the ground running, when push comes to shove ...'

'When the shit really hits the fan, you might get your water cut off ...'

'Keep up to snuff, have a gut feel ...'

'You've got to spend a buck to make a buck.'

Be careful, however, not to make a fool of yourself. I was told of a businessman who leapt up in the middle of an important meeting and declared:

'After a comfort break, I will tell you about my exposure problem.'

You should avoid that.

Cat Owners

I have to confess that there are no ready-to-hand phrases for cat owners. They are hardly necessary, however, as cat owners *never talk to each other*. They only talk to each other's cats, viz.:

'Puss, puss!'

It is nevertheless possible for cat owners to communicate with each other *provided that they talk through their cats*, e.g.:

'Someone got out of the wrong side of bed this morning, didn't she, coochee-coochee, tiddlums?'

'And who was it didn't feed you last night, silly old rat-face, isn't he ...?'

From my experience, cats are usually willing to let you do this and go along with it, if you give them a bit more to eat and a tummy-job.

Celebrities

Celebrities may be divided into two types (ah, there we go again.) There are those who say quaint things in order to give the impression of amiable eccentricity and there are those who *always say the same thing.* You must decide which type of celebrity you are going to be.

First, let us look at the celebrities who always say the same thing. Ken Dodd, the comedian, was quoted in the *Penguin Dictionary of Modern Quotations* as having been quoted in *The Times* (7 August 1965) saying:

> **'The trouble with Freud is that he never played the Glasgow Empire Saturday night.'**

In the *Observer* Colour Magazine (16 December 1984) he was quoted as saying:

> **'But Freud never played the second house at Glasgow Empire on a Friday night.'**

I know for a fact that Mr Dodd also made his remark on many other occasions in between these dates. What a superb record. Fancy keeping it up for almost twenty years. All celebrities can but envy such tenacity.

(One of these days I must ask Mr Dodd the reason for the subtle change from Saturday to Friday night. Also, why the addition of 'second house'? On reflection, I think this shows a flexible approach and is probably of no great importance.)

Take another celebrity: Mr Brian Redhead, that 'Prince of Broadcasters' as he has often been described. Talking about the Radio 4 *Today* programme to the London *Evening News* on 4 September 1978, he said:

> **'The *Today* programme is a unique opportunity to drop a word in the ear of the nation.'**

He told *Woman* on 10 December 1983:

> **'You want to drop a word in the ear of the nation, drop it during *Today*.'**

He told the *Sunday Times* on 9 December 1984:

> **'The point about *Today* is that if you want to get an idea into the ear of the nation, it is as good a programme as any.'**

A mere six year span, here, but very promising nevertheless. I think you will have got the point by now.

For celebrities who do not feel able to compete with these two famous wordsmiths, I would recommend the following very original things to say:

'I don't care what the papers say about me, as long as they say *something* and spell my name right.'

'All publicity is good publicity.'

'There's no such thing as bad publicity – only no publicity.'

'There's no such thing as over-exposure – only bad exposure.'

'You don't think I'm going to tell you what I earn, do you? But if you make it up, for heaven's sake make it big!'

What about celebs who wish to appear agreeably eccentric? Mr Ned Sherrin, wit and iconoclast, does this by letting his TV earpiece dangle, but this, unfortunately, is a technique outside the scope of this book.

Mr David Frost returned from Venice with his new wife and announced:

'We've been on a working honeymoon.'

Mr Richard Adams, the novelist famous for his charm, is given to telling interviewers:

'Have a wank, Frank.'

Mr Russell Harty, the former schoolteacher, has been known to utter the old Lancashire expression:

'I've knocked the odd nail in.'

(though quite what he means by this is anybody's guess.)

Celebrities should also compare themselves with other celebs, whenever possible. Britt Ekland announced of her liaison with Rod Stewart in 1977:

'We are really the Liz Taylor and Richard Burton of the 70s'

– though it is not recorded whether Liz Taylor and Richard Burton ever referred to themselves as the 'Britt Ekland and Rod Stewart of the 60s.'

Yoko Ono did, however, remark in 1984:

'John [Lennon] and I always thought, among other

things, that we were maybe the reincarnation of Robert and Liz.'

She was referring to Robert Browning and Elizabeth Barrett Browning. It is all very complicated. I wonder what the 'other things' they thought about were?

Mr Daley Thompson, the British athlete who won a gold medal in the decathlon in the 1984 Los Angeles Olympics, said:

'I haven't been so happy since my grandmother caught her tit in a mangle'

which caught exactly the right tone, surely?

Budding celebrities can develop these sayings to suit their own particular circumstances.

Centenarians

Whatever you say when you reach a hundred will be greeted with applause and telegrams from the Queen. People will be so amazed that you can say anything, let alone say it without falling over, that you will more or less be allowed to say what you want.

Nevertheless, when asked to give your secret for long life, you are well-advised to declare:

'I always drink a bottle of whisky a day'

and:

'I've been smoking forty a day since the age of fourteen.'

It is mandatory to say:

'If I'd known I was going to live this long, I'd have taken better care of myself.'

Adolph Zukor, the film producer, said it on his hundredth birthday. So, too, did the jazz musician, Eubie Blake, on *his*. Alas, Eubie died within five days, but there you go.

Children

It is not enough these days for children to go around reciting things like:

'Mrs Brown went to town
With her knickers hanging down.'

No, rather more sophistication is required. So children should practise the delivery of precocious, if not actually gnomic, bits of wisdom.

For example, of two women living together, they should ask:

'Are they Libyans?'

In this way their small talk will be collected by their parents and passed round for the delectation of their friends. Another good idea is for parents to keep an expensively-bound book in which to record these gems for the benefit of posterity.

Churchills

Those wishing to emulate the great Sir Winston Churchill have quite a task in front of them. Briefly, they should concentrate on a) jokes b) delivery and c) his little phrases.

The jokes are mostly of one type. You should arrange for a bishop to say to you, 'There are forty rooms in my palace!' Then, very quickly, you jump in with:

'And only Thirty-Nine Articles to put in them!'

This will have people rolling about on the floor in no time at all.

The nature of the delivery is too obvious to require elaboration here.

His little phrases include:

'Can a bloody duck swim?'

and:

'We must just K.B.O.!'

(This means 'Keep Buggering On' and helped raise the nation's morale when he used to say it every night on the radio during World War Two.)

Clergymen

The main thing about clergymen is that they should agree with God and say so as frequently as possible. Consider the following texts:

'Did you hear of the parson who began his sermon, **"As God said – and rightly ..."** '

(contained in the *Lyttelton-Hart-Davis Letters* for 1959)

'Consider what the Lord said to Moses – **and I think he was right ...**'

(from a BBC TV *That Was The Week That Was* sketch, 1963, delivered in a Field Marshal Montgomery voice)

'As Jesus said – **and how right he was ...**'

(Dr Donald Coggan, Archbishop of Canterbury, in a sermon at St Paul's to mark the Queen's Silver Jubilee, 1977)

Compare:

'St Paul says in one of his Epistles – **and I partly agree with him ...**'

(William Jackson, eminent clergyman at the beginning of the nineteenth century)

Need I say more?

When asked to say grace, clergymen should always choose words suited to the occasion. When the Reverend Sydney Smith, the nineteenth century wit, was asked to say grace he would look first to see whether champagne was on offer. If it was, he would begin:

'Oh, bountiful Jehovah!'

If it wasn't, he would pray:

'O Lord, we thank thee for even the least of thy benefits ...'

The Reverend David Bradford, a former journalist, said grace at the parliamentary lobby correspondents' centenary lunch in 1984, and began:

'Oh God, before whom all are attributable, make us truly thankful ...'

Go forth, and do thou likewise.

Calling on parishioners and finding them busy, clergymen should be prepared to fend off offers of tea with:

'Oh no, thank you, sherry will do ...'

Conjurors

As is well known, magicians and conjurors make a great show of letting audiences have a good look at the pieces of equipment they are about to use in their tricks. One such operative I saw (whose name, for the moment, unfortunately escapes me), came up with the following line when he was showing off the instrument with which he was going to saw his attractive lady assistant in half:

'The more you wave it about, the bigger it makes your act look.'

I have a feeling this line might also be useful in other contexts.

Otherwise, conjurors should say:

'Abracadabra'

a lot, and add, amusingly:

'Now, there's a name to conjure with!'

Criminals

See: POLICEMEN.

Culture Vultures

Appreciation of the arts requires the right words to express it. Opinions should always be expressed sufficiently loudly to be overheard by everybody else in the art gallery, museum, concert hall, or wherever.

One might think it unnecessary to go beyond the great Lord Clark's frequent ejaculation:

'What could be more agreeable ...?'

However, consider the following critical phrases:

'Not as good as the previous one ...'

'Like the curate's egg, it's good in parts ...'

'Goes from the sublime to gorblimey ...'

Special care should be taken with:

'Covent Garden this ain't ...'

Deaf People

See: WANTING TO STOP THE CONVERSATION.

Dentists

Dentists should remember to say:

'Just a little wider for me, please ...!'

– note thc 'for me', and:

'Another little rinse for me, please ...!'

– note the 'for me'.

In fact, it is best to let dentists do all the talking. It is, after all, sometimes impossible to say anything yourself when you mouth is stuffed full of cotton wool, drills and other bric-à-brac. Talking is probably the thing dentists are best at, anyway. I suppose it's all that looking down people's throats all day that does it. But they don't half go on. Looking down people's throats all day is also probably what gives rise to the high incidence of alcoholism in the dental profession.

Dog Owners

With dog owners, it is not so much *what* they say as *when* they say it that is important. What they say is:

'Down, Rover!'

or, occasionally:

'I don't think Mr —— likes you biting his ankle.'

But they must wait *at least twenty minutes* before saying either of these things. They should let their mastiffs slobber all over you, pong to high heaven, shove their snouts in your private parts, bark earth-shatteringly, and so on. They should pretend that it is perfectly possible to conduct an orderly conversation with you while this is going on. Only when you have been reduced to a pulp by the dreadful, smelly hound or when blood has actually been drawn (whichever is the sooner) should they use either of the two phrases.

Much the same applies to parents of children.

Dukes of Edinburgh

My advice is that Their Royal Highnesses the Dukes of Edinburgh should say:

'Bloody!'

and:

'Pull your finger out!'

rather a lot.

Editors

By editors, I really mean all senior executives in newspapers and broadcasting organizations, for they all talk much alike (when they're sober, that is.)

When they *are* sober they say awfully perceptive things – like the first 'editor' I had in Manchester who remarked, when I informed him I was leaving to go and work in London:

'Yes, I think we see you as more of a *Metropolitan* figure ...'

This can easily be adapted to suit almost any editorial occasion. For example, some miserable hack (*q.v.*) has just handed you a piece of copy. You should growl, spit, scratch, then aver:

'Lad, if you've never had your copy torn to shreds in

front of your face at three o'clock in the morning, you've never lived ...'

or muse, more mildly:

'Ah, yes, a very *Metropolitan* piece ...'

Incidentally, the editor who first used the 'Metropolitan' ploy on me was also the man who formed an in-house committee known as the Forward Outlook Group, or 'FOG', for short. You can see that he was a man to be reckoned with.

The chief aim of editors is not to be left 'with egg on the face' and to 'cover themselves' in the event of anyone complaining about their work.

They get their jobs by talking brilliantly and convincingly at appointments boards. For instance, the editor of a news programme on the wireless got the job after replying to the following questions from a BBC board, "How would you describe the sort of typical item you'll be looking for?' He replied in these words:

'I can't describe it. But when I hear it I'll know that I've got it.'

Broadcasting editors are for ever saying things like:

'I want knife-edge questioning'

and:

'Let's get a couple of MPs in and have a real ding-dong.'

Newspaper editors are nothing if not defensive. Either they don't want to be thought too elitist, in which case they reject material, saying:

'Not much for the punters in this, I don't think'

or, if they are accused of being too populist, say:

'We use long words here, you know – like "marmalade".'

But, as I say, they are usually too drunk to say anything. In which case their secretaries comment drily:

'After three o'clock in the afternoon, he transmits but doesn't receive.'

Fans

Having looked back through my fan mail over a number of

years, I am able to make a number of suggestions as to what goes down particularly well when dealing with someone you like and admire.

Once I was delighted to receive a card addressed to:

'Rees, the awful NOISE
Radio 4,
BBC,
London W1'.

Having made some innocuous comment about Peter Brook – to the effect that 'Whatever Peter Brook does is bound to be worth watching' – I rapidly received a fan letter describing this as:

'A compliment paid by a small nonentity to a big nonentity.'

Encouraged by this response, I said some other things. Reaction was not slow in coming:

'I recommend that, in future, you thoroughly rinse your mouth out with a good disinfectant before speaking on the radio.'

'I am constrained to warn you that your sarcastic and caustic remarks on biblical subjects ill become you – and these are heard by God – and "HE is not mocked" (Galatians 6:7). I'm truly sorry that such a nice person as you seem to be should take this risk – the ultimate consequences of which you must be wholly unaware.'

In due course, I involved myself with other people – Americans, even – in a programme which received a similarly warm reception:

'I find it exceedingly offensive because of the dirty-minded people taking part. *I wonder if their wives listen to it?*' [my italics]

'It is highly objectionable to have hideous-voiced smut-loving Americans brought into the programme but homosexuality is too *dreadful* an affliction to be the subject for "trying to be funny". **Are these unpleasant foreigners *paying* for their intrusion into *British* broadcasting? It is *more* than time this was put a stop to, and inquiries made ...'**

It really is very good of people to lash out on the stamp and send me this sort of stuff, especially when it is written with alternate lines in different coloured inks and underlined several times.

I have noticed, however, that when fans meet one in the flesh they change their tune – and never say nice things like this to one at all. Pity.

Ah, well. It is nice if they get your name almost right and don't confuse you with Gyles Brandreth.

Incidentally, it is less than good form to answer fans with printed cards of the 'Thank you for your inquiry but XXXX regrets that it is impossible for him to: read manuscripts/judge literary contests/answer questionnaires/donate copies of his books to libraries/give advice on how to start a literary career/etc.' variety. That sort of thing is best left to the likes of Bernard Shaw, Fritz Spiegl, Edmund Wilson and A.J.P. Taylor.

The only correct responses to enthusiasts who wish to share their manuscript or opinions with you were formulated a number of years ago by the excellent H.L. Mencken, when editor of the *American Mercury*.

Senders of unsolicited manuscripts were advised:

'Mr Mencken has just entered a Trappist monastery in Kentucky and **left strict instructions that no mail was to be forwarded. The enclosed is returned, therefore, for your archives.'**

Opinion-sharers were sent a postcard bearing the sympathetic message:

'Dear Reader,

You may be right.'

You will find this an extremely useful phrase to use in conversation, too.

Fatties

Fat women should say:

'I've got enough for all of you!'

(Claire Rayner has personally approved this.)

Guests

Dissatisfied guests may care to address their hosts with the words:

'I've had a wonderful evening – but this wasn't it.'

This brings the message home with pleasing warmth and zest.

Others may prefer to commit their comments to print – in the visitors' book. Morecambe and Wise are said to have written:

'We shall certainly tell our friends'

at theatrical digs they did not enjoy and John Barrymore simply inscribed:

'Quoth the Raven ...'

Hacks

I have written extensively in *The Joy of Clichés* about what newspaper and broadcast journalists should say. The only further thing that I would like to add on this subject is that they should also try and make use of the following delightful expressions whenever possible:

gentle giant: all tall people should be so described, especially dead policemen.

honeymoon is over for ——, the: the honeymoon is definitely *not* over for this wordsmith's helpmeet.

is there life after ——?: some excellent examples of this little-known form – 'Is there life after redundancy?' (*Sunday Times* Magazine, 14 October 1984) and 'Can there be life after Wogan?' (*Sunday People*, 14 October 1984.)

it was revealed last night: sounds so much better than 'another newspaper found this story and we are just copying it.'

just: planes should never have 'crashed twenty miles from the airport', they should always have 'crashed just twenty miles from the airport'. Rule: all distances are just. Further example: 'It is just 238,855 miles from the earth to the moon.'

like —— was going out of style: example – 'He was drinking champagne like money was going out of style.'

like there's no tomorrow: example – 'He was drinking champagne like there's no tomorrow.'

living life in the fast lane: 'controversial racing car genius Colin Chapman lived life in the fast lane' – Neil Wallis, 'Britain's Top Reporter', *Daily Star*, 11 October 1984.)

observers say: has so much more power and panache than 'me and my mates think'.

of all time: has to be one of the best journalistic phrases of all time.

so you think you can ——?: so you think you can be a popular journalist? Then use this phrase.

television cameras were filming: in fact, TV cameras don't use film. Only film cameras use film. TV cameras either televise (electronically) or record (electronically). This should not stop you from using the expression, however.

tells its own tale about the society we live in, this: so does this expression.

these are dynamite!: this is an expression members of the public always use when talking to newspapers, e.g.: 'Mr Little rushed to the Sun offices to study the photographs and said: "These are dynamite."' (*Sun*, 10 December 1984.)

under the glare of powerful arc-lamps: I am informed that arc-lamps went out years ago, but this should not stop you from using the expression.

whether ... remains to be seen: as in 'whether the President will change his mind and take the course I have just outlined at great length ... remains to be seen.' The alternative to this (to be employed especially by TV reporters standing outside the White House): **whether ... only time will tell.**

As this is basically a guide to *spoken* English, I should point out that these words and phrases all sound much better when repeated by a TV reporter standing in the middle of somewhere, wearing a warm coat and holding a microphone.

Old Fleet Street hacks should remind themselves that, long ago, when they joined newspapers, the preoccupations of their readers were encapsulated in the phrase:

'Tit, tote and television.'

Discuss.

Hairdressers

Like taxi-drivers, hairdressers already have the gift of the gab and need no further instruction.

However, they should no longer inquire of male customers:

'Will there be anything else, sir?'

– as this is no longer necessary.

Should they ever find themselves silent enough to think, they might like to mull over the following propositions that I have formulated for them:

1) Hairdressers always cut off too much of your hair. If they cut off less, you would have to go more often.
2) Often, the first time you go to a hairdresser, he does a wonderful job. The second time is never as good.
3) Having your hair cut means that it is going to rain.

Hoteliers

On the whole, hoteliers should only ever say one thing:

'I'm so sorry, I'll see to it right away.'

They then *don't do anything*. Or do something different. In this way, they have the last laugh.

Hoteliers should also pretend not to hear you when you request a double bed. They should give you twin beds instead.

A year or two ago my wife and I went to stay in a recommended hotel in the middle of Wales. It was in the

Good Food Guide and the *Good Hotel Guide* – quite apart from which someone had told us it actually *was* good. Of course, the first thing we noticed when we were shown into our room was two single beds when we had specifically requested a double bed. After half an hour or so of husbandly hoo-ing and haa-ing and 'Do you really want to make a fuss about it?' and 'It doesn't make that much difference, really, does it?' sort of thing on my part, I had to steel myself for a visit to Reception:

ME: 'Oh, sorry to trouble you, but I think we did ask for a double bed and ... um ... we seem by mistake, I'm sure, to have been given ... um ... two singles ...'

PROPRIETOR: 'Yes.'

ME: 'Well, you see, it's not quite what we asked for. Two instead of one. Not quite the same, is it?'

PROPRIETOR: 'I see.'

ME: 'Um ... we were wondering if you could do anything about it?'

PROPRIETOR: 'Not straight away. They're up on the roof.'

ME: 'I beg your pardon? What are? The beds?'

PROPRIETOR: 'The men.'

ME: 'Ah. I see ... Sounds as if it's going to be rather a lot of trouble.'

PROPRIETOR: 'Yes, it will be.'

ME: 'Well, perhaps you could do what you can ... Thank you.'

And that is where I left it, nurturing no real hope of success. The wife and I went off for a walk and when we came back the two single beds were still there. At that point we rather gave up on anything being done.

When we came back to our room after dinner, surprise, surprise, there was a whopping big double bed. 'Take back all I said', etc.

It was only when we were inside it that we realized that it was not a double bed at all. Nor was it two single beds shoved side by side lengthwise, as sometimes happens. It was two single mattresses shoved side by side breadthwise, on a double bed base. This had the virtue of one's not falling down the middle between the mattresses. Instead it sort of opened up and one's bottom did.

Last laugh, as I said.

Interviewers

These people were dealt with in considerable depth in *The Joy of Clichés*. However, among the questions suggested in that book for keeping broadcast conversations bubbling along, there were seven important omissions which I should now like to rectify.

The first concerns the interviewing of song-smiths – A. Lloyd Webber, O. Hammerstein, W.S. Gilbert, and the like. It is absolutely mandatory to ask such people:

'Which gets written first – the words or the music?'

The second must be addressed to actors who appear on stage on both sides of the Atlantic. They should always be asked:

'Do you find that audiences in Britain are different to those in America?'

(You will usually find that they can say something about this.)

The third is that unusual question:

'What was your first big break?'

The fourth:

'Was that a turning point in your career?'

The fifth:

'What do you think your book is about?'

The sixth:

'How has being famous changed your life?'

And, seventh:

'Out of all the many, many ——, do you have a particular favourite?'

It is important to save up this question to the end of the interview, as the interviewee may not have had a chance of mentioning it till then. If he has already mentioned it, he'll just have to think of another one quickly.

Useful ploys to get the best out of your guests include:

1) mangling the title of the book they have written
2) asking them the same question twice.

Since I have opened up this subject again, I might as well hand on a useful tip to radio and TV interviewers who suddenly find themselves having to interview somebody *when they have absolutely no idea why*. This happens more often than you might think. In the early days of LBC, Britain's first commercial radio station, I had to present a three hour breakfast show on Saturdays and Sundays, seemingly without the benefit of a producer's services. To fill time I would quite often say, 'Ah, the *Sunday Times* has an interesting report this morning ...' – and read it out. But that is not the advice I would give. No, I am thinking of the time when I was handed a note scribbled on the back of an envelope saying that Ernest Marples, a Conservative politician of yesteryear, was coming in to be interviewed at 8.15 a.m. It did not say why. I was so busy chattering away, putting on commercials, and pedalling the dynamo, that I had no time to chat to him before he was wheeled into the studio to begin the interview. And so I began:

'Good morning, Mr Marples, it's a big day for you ...?'

He, thank goodness, replied to the effect that it was the tenth anniversary of something to do with the Channel Tunnel, or the M1, or some such matter, and we were away. So, there you have it, a gambit to remember.

It does not strictly lie within the scope of this guide but, since this section seems to be rattling along nicely, I must add a cautionary word about interviewers' questions which, accidentally or on purpose, are designed to render the interviewee momentarily speechless.

I have been on the receiving end of such questions on two occasions. I was once being interviewed on television about graffiti, a subject on which I can speak for many hours without notes, when Jenni Murray, the charming interviewer, asked me in her best Robin Day manner:

'And, tell me, have *you* ever done it in a lavatory?'

Another time, I was touring Australia, giving interviews on the same topic (see GUESTING ON CHAT SHOWS), and was beginning to wonder whether I would ever get asked an *original* question on graffiti. Then, one morning in an Adelaide radio station, I was. The interviewer asked me:

'And, Nigel, is there a *season* for graffiti?

What did this mean? Did he suppose there was a sort of rutting season for graffiti-writers, that when the sap rose they reached for their spray-cans? I cannot, off-hand, recall my answer.

The pre-eminent arena in Britain for this sort of questioning has, for many years, been the Radio 4 breakfast-time *Today* programme. Its famous host once was Jack de Manio who, apart from being unable to tell the time, could also bowl verbal googlies. In the early days of the troubles in Northern Ireland (about 1969), it was known as a 'civil rights' dispute. One morning, Jack was ploughing through a list of prepared questions and putting them to some worthy Ulsterman, when his own, natural, curiosity made him wonder about the phrase 'civil rights'. He asked:

'And how many coloured people are there in Northern Ireland?'

Unfortunately, off-hand, I can't remember the reply he got, either.

Also on the *Today* programme, when I was introducing it, I remember an item we had about a man who raised buff Orpingtons, a breed of poultry. He had devoted much of his life to this hobby but in his middle years he had found time to take unto himself a wife. For the honeymoon, they went, and this, as far as I can tell at this distance, was the point of the story, to Orpington. The blushing bride and groom were interviewed at home against a background of clucking buff Orpingtons. All proceeded merrily until the interviewer ventured to ask the bride:

'And when you were on your honeymoon, did he show you his buff Orpingtons?'

As I say, you have to be terribly careful with this sort of thing.

Judges

Although I cannot imagine many of my readers falling into this category, it is nevertheless very important that judges should always have enough to say. It would be a tragedy for British justice if they were ever to shut up.

It is difficult, of course, to give precise guidance – apart from the obvious use of such perfectly reasonable queries as:

'And who, pray, are the Beatles?'

or interesting autobiographical statements like:

'I have not travelled by tram since 1932'

– but the main point is that judges should always be charming, witty and fair in whatever they say.

It is outside the scope of this book to suggest whether they should also cultivate their appearances to the extent of looking like death warmed up.

The following real-life examples should guide you in the right direction:

'Wife beating may be socially acceptable in Sheffield, but it is a different matter in Cheltenham.'

Lord Justice Lawton

'You might like to know that I've just been informed that Australia are four for one.'

Judge Alan King-Hamilton, during the Gay News *trial at the Old Bailey, 1977.*

'[Your verdict is] remarkably merciful in the light of the evidence.'

Judge Alan King-Hamilton, 1979, when a jury acquitted defendants on conspiracy and arms charges.

'It strikes me as being one of the kind of accidents that could almost happen to anyone.'

Judge Brian Gibbens, 1983, during the trial of a man accused of having intercourse with a little girl (he later claimed he was misreported in The Times*).*

'I wish these people would show more efficiency about these overdoses. How much trouble they would save.'

Judge Bertrand Richard, 1983, on a man who had attempted to commit suicide by taking a drug overdose.

When it comes to what ordinary mortals should say to judges, one can but point to the excellent example set by the late Mr Marty Feldman during the *Oz* trial in 1970:

'Am I speaking loud enough for you, judge?'

and:

'Sorry, am I waking you up?'

Married People

Having achieved the marital state relatively late in life, I am afraid I have no suggestions as to what married persons should say beyond the excellent, clarion cry I first noticed married people using in my bachelor days. Either partner can say it, and it goes:

'Have you got the keys, darling?'

There is not a lot more to marriage than saying this.

Nannies

Few professionals have built up such an array of verbal lore as nannies. Handed on from generation to generation, perhaps even taught at nanny schools nowadays, these pearls are an essential part of technique.* They are also useful to those who seek to emulate nannies in other fields (e.g. prime ministers, directors-general of the BBC, etc.)

At my request, Lord Lucan has personally selected his favourites. And here they are:

'Somebody got out of bed the wrong side today.'
'You have made your bed and now you must eat it.'
'A dry bed deserves a boiled sweet.'
'You'd be late for your own funeral.'
'Back in the knife box, little miss sharp.'

* Two books – *The Rise and Fall of the British Nanny*, Jonathan Gathorne-Hardy, (Hodder & Stoughton, 1972) and *Nanny Says*, Sir Hugh Casson and Joyce Grenfell (Dobson Books, 1972) – contain pages of advice to the aspiring.

'If wishes were horses, beggars could ride.'
'Save your breath to cool your porridge.'
'Fish is good for the brains.'
'Think of all the poor starving people in Africa.'
'You must wear clean underwear in case you get run over.'
'Cat got your tongue?'
'There's more ways of killing a cat than choking it with cream.' (See also PROVERBS.)
'Cold hands, warm heart.'
'The nicest things come in the smallest parcels.'
'Queen Anne's dead.'

When asked by their charges how old they are, nannies should reply:

'A little older than my teeth and as old as my tongue.'

Office Workers

Office personnel should remember that they are not there to be helpful. Let that be clearly understood. They exist to count paperclips, indulge in feuds and banter, and generally to fill the time until their next holidays as well as they possibly can. This approach can best be summed up by the notice:

'We do *NOT* give facilities for change, telephone books, or anything not pertaining to this business.'

Useful phrases when fobbing off requests include:

'It's more than my job's worth ...'
'I love you, too!' (telephonic encounters).

Office personnel should also resort to the use of initials whenever possible. Thus:

'T.G.I.F.' means 'Thank God, it's Friday.'
'P.O.E.T.S. day' also means Friday ('Piss off early, tomorrow's Saturday.)
– not forgetting **'T.I.S.W.A.S.'** ('Today is Saturday, wear a smile.')

Above all, they should use a *particular* type of lingo. How one would describe it, I don't know – all I can do is to give some examples of the sort of thing that office personnel should always say:

'Cheer up. You'll soon be dead!'
'... well, as near as damn is to swearing.'
'I'll be with you in two shakes of a lamb's tail ...'
'Quicker than winking ...'
'There's one born every minute!'
'Bless your little cotton socks!'
'Don't scratch it, you'll only make it worse!'

The careful use of these phrases, after study, must surely lead to greater productivity.

Old People

When I say 'old people', I really mean people who are conscious of their age. This condition usually begins any time after the age of thirty-five. Such people should start saying things like:

'I wasn't born yesterday, you know'

or:

'I was born in nineteen hundred and frozen to death'

or:

'Nineteen hundred and mind your own business.'

They should also evoke:

'If only we could recreate that wonderful spirit there was in the war'

and:

'Corporal punishment? Well, it never did us any harm, did it?'

Very much what old people should be saying, that one.

Operatives

Operatives, whether they be garage mechanics, builders or plastic surgeons, should always begin by saying:

'Who put that in for you?'

– because they are basically in the estimating and fixing

business. Consequently, they will already be past masters at the gentle art of drawing in the breath between the teeth at any suggestion made to them. In fact, short intakes of breath are more likely to get results than actually saying anything.

However, a friend of mine tells of a builder who was carrying out very extensive work for him and who said something very reassuring indeed.

'You know that estimate we talked about, Mr White?' he began (note the careful use of 'talked about' rather than 'agreed'.)

'Yes, yes,' said my friend.

'Well, "24", I think we was talking about?'

'Yes, yes,' said my friend.

'Well, I thought I'd better warn you, what with one thing and another, that it now looks as though it will be nearer to "32" ...'

'Ah, "32", eh?' said my friend. 'I wonder, could you be a bit more specific? How much nearer will it be to "32"?'

'Er, well,' replied the operative, 'Not to put too fine a point on it, and what with one thing and another, "46".'

Brilliant. This example shows word-mastery of a very special kind and yet it can be learned very quickly with the aid of this book.

Parents

See: DOG OWNERS.

People Who Can't Pronounce Their Rs

Have you noticed how people with speech impediments always try and make life difficult for themselves? People with stutters invariably throw in those useless little phrases like 'Don't you kn-kn-kn-kn-kn-know, old th-th-th-thing?' and 'If you kn-kn-kn-kn-know wh-wh-wh-wh-what I m-m-m-m-ean?' which it would be so much easier to leave out.

Similarly, people who can't pronounce their Rs, rather than take the obvious course and omit all words containing the letter R from their conversation, almost always put more of them in and *draw attention* to them.

I am thinking of that distinguished politician Roy ('Woy') Jenkins who rarely lets slip an opportunity to say:

'Vewy agweeable'

and that excellent broadcaster Brian Walden (or Bwian Ralden, as he is known to the Chinese). I still recall with delight his description of the challenger in the 1980 American Presidential Election as:

'Pwesident Carter's Wepublican Wival, Wonald Weagan.'

As this adds to the gaiety of nations, I can see no real harm in it.

Photographers

Photographers have to keep it up. They have to keep on burbling away, 'That's it, look at me, moisten your lips, just a little bit wider with the legs, that's it darling, yeh, sensational', etc.

However, to get the requisite grin they should say either:

1) **'Watch the birdie.'**

2) **'Say "Cheese".'**

or, much better, adopt Cecil Beaton's command:

3) **'Say "Lesbian".'**

Look where it got him.

Policemen

Do you know what the three-headed policeman said to the criminal? Well:

''Ello, ello, ello, what's all this then?'

What's more, they really do, you know. I was once walking peacefully down the Cornmarket in Oxford when a bunch of punks – perhaps, it is true, somewhat affected in their behaviour because they were 'carrying certain substances' – were set upon by a bunch of thugs, i.e. policemen, who were also carrying certain substances, i.e. large bunches of keys, walkie-talkies, notebooks, etc., all stuffed somewhat inelegantly in their trouser pockets.

I was intrigued to hear what they actually said when shoving the punks into their van:

''Ere mate, you're nicked!'

They really did say that. Presumably, they were taught it at Hendon.

Other standard phrases, police persons, for the use of include:

'I have you bang to rights.'

'None of your lip.'

'Breath into this bag, if you'd be so kind.'

'Pull the other one, sunshine, it has bells on it.'

'I'm a bit hazy on the details, but ...'

'On your merry way, then, sharpish ...'

When beating a suspect black and blue, suggest:

'You play ball with me, chummy, and I'll play ball with you ...'

My own, personal, contact with the boys in blue has, of course, been eminently peaceable. I once had a P.C. Pode round from Kentish Town nick to give my dwelling a Crime Prevention visit. 'D'you ever leave a window open when you go out?' he inquired. 'Yes,' I replied, 'one doesn't want to come back to a stuffy flat, does one?' Averred he:

'Better a stuffy flat than a burgled one, as we say in the force.'

Criminals, depending on their class, need only say:

'I dunno what you're talking about'

or:

'But, officer, there must be some mistake ...'

or:

'Somebody must have been lacing my drinks ...'

or:

'I don't think you realize who I am, Inspector. I am a very good friend of the Home Secretary'

even if they end up having to say:

'It's a fair cop, guv.'

Innocent members of the public should always round off the whole affair by asking:

'There's just one thing I don't understand, inspector ...?'

and he, of course, will tell them.

Pop Stars

Well, there are so many things pop stars can say. I would draw especial attention, however, to what the Everly Brothers said when they played at Wembley Arena in 1984.

One of them, Don or the other one, said:

'It's just such a privilege to be here at Wembleyonthe-outskirtsofLondon.'

I wondered at the time whether he thought that 'WembleyontheoutskirtsofLondon' was the name of the place?

Public Speakers

Exhaustively covered in *The Joy of Clichés*, this subject has recently been adorned with the addition of another handful of new, golden phrases:

1) **'Thus far and no further.'**
2) **'Too little, too late.'**
3) **'Get them off the front-burner.'**
4) **'These people whom you mention'** (i.e. opponents).
5) **'... I hear you cry.'** (As in, 'When is the Government going to get off its backside? – I hear you cry.')

Publishers

When rejecting your best-selling novel or whatever, clever publishers invariably say:

'We cannot find a place for it in our list *at this time*.' [My italics]

Note two things about this statement. They are not telling you your book is a load of rubbish: they are merely breaking it to you that it doesn't fit their list – not much of a snub, when you consider the rest of the list. Also, there is no place for it 'at this time'. This is a convenient cover for them, when it is accepted by another publisher and becomes the all time best-seller out-selling *The Country Diary of an Edwardian Lady*. They can then say that they liked the book but rejected it because it wasn't suitable *at the time* it was offered to them.

Should your manuscript be accepted, though, you will have to put up with other publishers' sayings. If you tell them you have not been able to find your treasured tome in any bookshops, they will tell you:

'Well, it must have sold out …'

If you ask them, 'Is it selling well?' they will reply:

'Yes, it is selling well.'

This completely neglects to mention that it is selling well *into* shops but not necessarily *out* of them. If copies remain unsold in bookshops, the publisher will take them back and they will not be counted as sales on your royalty statement. They all do this. You can never get them out of the habit of saying this. All publishers should follow suit.

Quizmasters

Radio and TV quizmasters should never say 'Yes' to the answers they are given. They should invariably say:

'Absolutely right!'

At the start of their programmes they should always say:

'The rules are very simple'

and:

'You'll pick them up as we go along.'

(Ted Rogers once said that about *3-2-1*.)

Real Bread Campaigners

All this talk about high-fibre diets, bran-with-everything cooking, lentil blow-outs, and so on, has, if nothing else, made it easier to deal with certain aspects of, er, personal hygiene, if I can put it like that. I mean, that *F-Plan Diet* woman (the one who made all the money) had her readers, well, not to put too fine a point on it, looking at it after they'd done it. Life is getting very difficult these days, if healthier, I suppose.

Still, what I'm getting round to is the man I once interviewed on the radio about Real Bread. In the wake of Real Beer and Real Cheese these bread-makers ganged together to make sure there was nobody left in Islington eating that nasty white sliced spongy stuff. Everybody had to eat that brown, wholemeal, not-a-great-deal-of-fun and sticks-between-your-teeth variety.

Anyway, the man in question had brought along a sample of Real Bread for me to taste. My immediate reaction was that it was, to put it mildly, rather tough on the old gnashers. A bit chewy. A bit *al dente* (as they used to say in the *Good Food Guide* before it went downmarket).

I pointed this out to the chap and he, completely unperturbed, said:

> 'Ah, yes, glad you noticed that. Well, it's like we say, **"Hard In, Soft Out"**.'

Millions of listeners must have been as impressed by this slogan as I was, and I have been trying to find a suitable conversation to drop it into ever since.

Royal Commentators

You know those deferential little reports they have on the TV news about the comings and goings of members of the Royal Family? Well, these are not compiled without a great deal of work on the part of reporters, who have the difficult job of pretending to stand up straight while in fact crouching on one knee.

This is not the place to go too deeply into their work, as their conversations with the viewer are invariably one-sided, but I thought I might just mention the ever-useful:

'The Queen Mother clearly enjoyed herself'

– even if her expression was rather less scrutable than this supposes. It is, simply, what one always says.

Few commentators, or chatterers, about Royalty will ever, I am afraid, hope to rise to the heights scaled by Mr Tom Fleming at a Royal occasion in 1977. As the procession swept before his gaze, he mused:

'One wonders what the conversation will be in the stable tonight when these horses get home?'

The quintessence, surely?

Scotsmen

Of course, all Scotsmen should say 'Jimmy!' and 'Och aye, the noo!' at every opportunity, though only in the presence of Sassenachs. But there is also one little thing they can do, and Glasgow taxi-drivers are past masters at it, to make the visitor feel at home. It all hinges on the fact that to the Scotsman the word 'stay' means 'live'. I always forget this. Hence, the following fragment of conversation recorded in a cab between Glasgow Airport and the city:

DRIVER: **'Do ye stay in Glasgee?'**
ME: 'Er … only for the one night.'
DRIVER: 'Oh, so ye don't then …'
ME: '… Mrrmph?'

To the Scots this makes up for any amount of ribbing about moths in their wallets.

Showbiz Folk

It is not just enough for showbiz folk to say:

'Rhubarb, rhubarb'

and:

'It'll be all right on the night'

(or 'alright' as they say it at London Weekend Television) and:

'Break a leg!'

on first nights. Oh no. When recalling the good old days (something they do a lot), they should evoke:

'... Those great music-hall days when there weren't any microphones or any of this modern amplification and yet you could stand right at the back of the circle **... and not hear a bleeding word!'**

When recalling old songs, they should comment:

'They don't write songs like that any more!'

(as well as adding:)

'... thank goodness!'

When recalling old shows, they should say:

'I did audition for *Oh, Calcutta!* but the part was too small.'

When recalling an uproarious or disastrous incident, they should cap it by saying:

'Follow that with the sea-lions!'

On no account should they say, 'There wasn't a dry eye in the house.' Always:

'There wasn't a dry seat in the house.'

An actor's life consists of setting himself up to be rejected. Hence the ready selection of phrases he has for this:

'He gave me the frozen mit.'

'They gave her the Big E' (i.e. 'elbow').

A showbiz person is also hard to comfort ('No need to make a song and dance about it!') In real life, there is a saying: 'What are the three most useless things in the world? Answer: a nun's cunt, the Pope's balls, and a vote of thanks.' The entertainer adapts this to:

1) 'A nun's tits.

2) 'The Pope's balls.

3) 'A rave review in *The Stage.*'

Most of showbiz is pretty tacky, so two things get said pretty frequently:

'Darling, I cried all the way to the bank.'

'Darling, I should take the money and run.'

My advice is to keep as far away from these people as you can, darling.

Siblings

Big brothers and sisters should say:

'I'm bigger than you'

and when a little brother or sister is unwise enough to say, 'I want ...';

' "I want" doesn't get.'

Sob Sisters

Otherwise known as Agony Aunts. If these are Claire Rayner, the solution to every problem is:

'Have a good cry, luv.'

(Sometimes the location for this good cry is specified – usually the loo.)

If they are Anna Raeburn and are dealing with Terry from Highgate who is speaking from a call-box and can't get it up, the solution to the problem is:

'Brace up! And have a good cold shower.'

Spies

Spies are extraordinarily silly people who should be encouraged to play their pathetic little games and blow each other up, as this helps keep them from interfering with the lives of ordinary folk. Who cares whether our country's pathetic secrets get leaked to the Russians? They probably know them anyway.

If spies do want to have secret passwords and the like, they would do best to say things like:

'Knock three times and ask for ——'

or use the exchange perfected by Geoffrey Prime. In reply to a contact saying, 'I believe we met in Pittsburgh in 1968', Prime was to reply:

'No, at that time I was in Berlin.'

That'll do, and if you must say these things, don't be put off by the fact that Prime got thirty-five years for it.

Taxi-Drivers

Heaven forbid that one should put any more words in the mouths of those already so coruscatingly and brilliantly crammed with them. However, taxi-drivers might care to perfect their technique in a) the **'I know where it is but I just can't place it'** routine and b) the **'I had … in the back of the cab last week'** rhapsody.

The point about a) is that no attempt should be made to look the address up in the taxi-driver's *A-Z* (given the remote chance that he has one) as this spoils the fun; and b) that this should never contain complimentary material. 'I had that Meryl Streep in the back o' me cab last week, guv. Knew straight away even though she had no make-up on. Very bad complexion. Know that? It's amazing, in'it? … Er, 'scuse me, guv, did I see you on *Wogan* the other week?'

Teachers

Teachers are well advised to emulate the former adviser for spoken English in Mid-Glamorgan, John Edwards, and say things like:

> **'There's far too much sex in this school and I'm not having any of it …'**
>
> **'Look at the blackboard while I go through it.'**

When talking to parents about their children, teachers must never so much as mention the prospect of little Johnny failing. They should refer instead to the 'de-stimulus of non-achievement'.

All teachers should equip themselves with twitchy mannerisms, funny voices – and catchphrases. In my childhood I had a female teacher who would always say:

> **'Come along cherubs, chickabiddies and … oh, I've forgotten what the other one is again …'**

without fail. I'm still not sure what she was talking about. That's the sort of thing.

On the question of corporal punishment, they should say things like:

'Boy! Bend over! I have here two slippers – one called "Percy" and the other called "Mercy". **I have decided to beat you with "Percy" – that is to say, "Without Mercy"!'**

Teachers of religion should be prepared for questions along the lines of, 'Please, sir, what's a harlot?' They should answer:

'A woman who sells her body for money.'

The disappointed 'Yes, sir …' will be reward enough.

Tourists

Not to be confused with travellers, of course. The difference has been well delineated in the saying:

'I am a traveller, you are a tourist and they are trippers.'

Tourists are always American, anyway, and should limit themselves to the following complimentary remarks:

'I came to London to find the streets paved with gold.'

'It was wonderful and a rare privilege to visit with you …'

'The delicious dinner at the quaint old pub was truly a rare treat and quite different …'

'Our tour was unique …'

'You afforded us such a rare opportunity and the evening went all too quickly …'

'We'll be looking forward to rolling out the red carpet for you …'

They should reserve criticism for the airline that brought them over and for their own home town:

'—— is the arsehole of the world,'

they should say,

'and —— is half-way up it.'

When Brits exclaim, 'Bob's your uncle!' tourists should pretend not to know this old expression and say, with a straight face:

'But how did you know? I *do* have an uncle called Bob …'

Welshmen

Welshmen should say:

'Boyo!'

as often as possible and speak English to each other. They should start speaking Welsh only when an Englishman approaches.

Part 2
What To Say To ...

Acquaintances

There is, of course, a distinction between 'acquaintances' and 'friends'. Acquaintances are friends you haven't made yet and about whom you are not too sure. Hence, you promise to 'give them a bell'. This, as promises go, carries about as much weight as the injunctions:

'Let's keep in touch!'

and:

'We must have lunch sometime ...'

Authors

It is important not to confuse one author with another. Writers are notoriously sensitive people and very much resent being congratulated on the works of another.

You are on reasonably safe ground, however, if you tread cautiously where any criticism is concerned. Try:

'Is it my imagination or was your first book a better one?'

That ought to break the ice.

Equally likely to go down well when the author exclaims, 'You don't mean you actually *bought* a copy?' is:

'No, I'm afraid, I got it out of the library'

or:

'No, the Book Club sent it ... I didn't really want it, you see.'

Another question likely to get authors on your side is:

'Do you just do your writing – or have you got a proper job?'

Foreigners

There are no special phrases to be addressed to foreigners. Don't waste your time with any of that '*Dov'è il consolato Britannico?*' nonsense. They must make do with ordinary English. The one concession you may make to them is to speak English slowly and in a VERY LOUD voice. This way, they usually understand.

Should you be travelling in America and people start to gather round listening to you incredulously and saying, 'Dig that accent!' – do not lose your dignity but reply, simply:

'What accent? You're the people with the accent!'

In Texas, however, you should explain:

'I'm from *East* Texas.'

Unaccountably, this makes them fall about laughing.

Gays

These people should be humoured. The best line to put to them to open up the conversation is:

'How's trade?'

or:

'What a gay day!'

but not:

'Like a nice time, dearie?'

It is considered impolite to exclaim:

'Backs to the walls, chaps!'

or:

'I'll see you behind the bike sheds after school'

or to describe how a certain person got a job:

'He bent over in the shower at Eton.'

(Cf. the admonition:

'Don't drop your car keys!'

and the Irish expression:

'If you drop a fiver in Bandon, kick it all the way to Cork.')

Equally, the lines:

'Camp as a row of tents'

'Queer as a clockwork orange'
'Bent as a nine bob note'
'Queen for a day'
and:
'There's nowt so queer as folk'
are best reserved for other contexts.

Hecklers

When making a public speech, it is vitally important to be able to respond to hecklers. They are usually pretty uninspiring people, often with spots, limiting themselves to such stock phrases as 'Resign!' or 'What about the workers?' The simplest technique is to agree with them, as this disarms them completely (rather like saying 'Oh, yes, why don't you come in?' to Jehovah's Witnesses.)

I recall an excellent example of this technique demonstrated by Mr Robert Morley, the thespian, at the Oxford Union. He was speaking in a debate on private v. state education and started slagging off his old school, viz. Marlborough. Provoked by this, a member of the audience, and presumably a fellow Old Marlburian, called out, 'Shame!' Morley, quick as a flash, agreed: 'Yes, it was the most frightful shame. I don't know how I ever put up with it.' Collapse of shamed party.

What it is vital not to do is lose your rag. There are numerous instances of this, alas. Bob Hope began his long decline when interrupted by feminist demonstrators during a Miss World Contest at the Royal Albert Hall. He found it hard not to liken them to the Vietcong. He also, and this was unforgiveable, ordered a minion to skip a few idiot boards in order to hasten the end of his act.

More recently, the Rt. Hon. Cecil Parkinson, the well-known Conservative father-figure, was poised to make a political comeback. Speaking on the subject of student grants at a Tory dinner at Warwick University, he was heckled by someone shouting, 'You should know all about being a parent ...'

Parkinson lost his rag. 'You don't even have the right to talk to me, you little rat,' he said, putting a damper on the whole proceedings. How much better if he had light-heartedly agreed?

People Who Leave The Door Open

You should say to these inconsiderate people either:

'Are there no doors in your house?'

or:

'Were you born in a barn/
in a field/
in a pub with swing doors/
on a raft?'

That is what they say in the best circles, anyway.

Pianists

My maternal grandmother always knew how to compliment a pianist when she saw one. First of all, she invariably twisted his arm and got him to play something. She would then pass judgement on the piano, using the words:

'It's got a lovely *tone*.'

Next she would praise the pianist – though never to his face. She would say:

'He's got a lovely *touch*.'

This is the way to do it.

Plagiarists

This is not an area I know a great deal about, frankly. Nevertheless, it has been brought to my attention what very irate people who think their works have been plagiarized ought to say – and usually do.

They say things like:

'At the risk of sounding frightfully pompous, I must say

that the material has been stolen just as surely as if someone had walked into the house and taken a wad of notes off the kitchen dresser'

and:

'Something must be done to remove the odour of stinking fish.'

When a settlement has been reached, the injured party asks:

'Can you arrange for the money to be sent direct to Oxfam?'

because:

'If you send me the money direct, it gives me all sorts of trouble with the tax people.'

I hope such people won't mind my quoting them, but it does seem to be very good stuff.

Radio And TV Interviewers

Should you ever chance to be interviewed on radio or TV, you should take a leaf from the book of Conservative Members of Parliament. They are trained how to be interviewed and they are also quite clearly taught what to say to the interviewer after it is all over, viz:

'I thought you handled that very well'

and:

'Thank you for making it so painless.'

(If they are not taught to say these things, then they must just have very good manners, because they always do say them.)

Authors plugging their books should say, after the interview:

'It's so nice to meet someone who's actually read the book!'

or:

'You've obviously done your research.'

This always produces an interesting reaction.

Smelly People

There is not a lot that you can do with such people as they seem impervious to the dropping of hints. It may be in vain, but you can always try:

'Phew! Cottage cheese!'

or:

'Phew! Armpits!'

Smokers

If you are a non-smoker, and, of course, you are these days, you should waste no time in ridiculing those who persist in the evil habit:

'Oh, not one of the minority, are you?'

you should say, or:

'Oh, I'm so sorry, I thought for a funny moment that somebody was smoking in here, but then I thought, surely, no one could be so foolish ...'

If that fails to work, then try the more direct:

'Don't you find it makes your clothes smell?'

This sort of thing will soon let them know how you feel about their filthy ways.

Should anyone be so foolish as to ask, 'Do you mind if I smoke?' your reply is:

'I don't care if you burst into flames!'

Unfortunately, despite all the giant strides in shutting off cinemas, Tube trains, and so on, to smokers, there is still one area where miserable smokers do tend to congregate in large numbers.

I am talking about restaurants *where I happen to be eating*. I look around at the other tables and – *at every one* – there are people coughing and retching over their cigarettes. Why is this? Is there some correlation between smoking and stuffing the mouth with restaurant food? Or have restaurants become the last refuge of the smoker?

One mustn't lose one's cool, of course. Therefore I am grateful to an erstwhile chief inspector of the *Good Food*

Guide who tells me what to say when a person is smoking at the next table to you. Ask politely:

'Would you be so kind as to hold the cigarette in your other hand?'

This apparently has a devastatingly unsettling effect and is the equivalent of saying:

'Put that in your pipe and smoke it.'

Ugly Women

You should say to them:

'Put them back on again!'

or:

'Excuse me, but didn't you win the Derby in 1956?'

Unwanted Guests

First recorded, I think, by G.W.E. Russell in his *Collections and Recollections* (1898), was a helpful remark of Dr Vaughan, Head Master of Harrow, designed to get rid of boys he had entertained at breakfast. 'When the muffins and sausages had been devoured ... and all permissible school-topics discussed, there used to ensue a horrid silence ... Then the Doctor would approach with cat-like softness, and, extending his hand to the shyest and most loutish boy, would say,

"Must you go? Can't you stay?"

and the party broke up with magical celerity.' It was later twisted to:

'Must you stay? Can't you go?'

and attributed to Dr Butler, Master of Trinity College, Cambridge.

The painter Sickert once said to Denton Welch, his visitor:

'Come again when you can't stay so long ...'

Welch commented, in a *Horizon* article (1942): 'At these words a strange pang went through me, for it was what my father had always said as he closed the book, when I had finished my bread and butter and milk, and it was time for bed.'

Still recommended.

If you get no results even from this, stand up and say to your guests:

'Haven't you got a home to go to?'

or, as in the case of the duke who was imposed upon by a Royal visitor:

'Don't these people have palaces to go to?'

Vicars

After the service, it is permitted to say to the vicar:

'I must say, what a wonderful sermon you preached this morning! **If only you could give one like that *every* Sunday you'd really be getting somewhere!'**

Should you have an opportunity to welcome a vicar into your home, say:

'Take a pew!'

Should you have a disagreement with one, reassure him with:

'I believe you, but thousands wouldn't!'

Part 3

What to Say In *Any* Situation

Conversation Glue

There are certain useful phrases which can be inserted into absolutely any conversation and which will help to keep it rattling along without distracting too much from the general drift. First, there are one- or two-word 'talk lubricants' such as:

'Anyway ...'
'Meanwhile ...'
'And finally ...'
'Like the man said ...'
'As the poet said ...'
'And so on ...'

and so on.

Then there are rather more colourful expressions which fulfil a similar purpose in conversational exchanges. For example:

A: 'I say, old fellow, how long can this government survive, do you think?'
B: **'How long is a piece of string?!'**
A: 'But they really are in the most desperate pickle ...'
B: **'Nothing that a cup of tea won't put right!'**

The beauty of this kind of phrase is that it enables you to join in the conversation without necessarily agreeing with the person who is making all the running. Consider also using:

'Variety is the spice of life ...'
'No wonder there's been a change in the weather ...!'
'How high is a Chinaman ...?!'
'Worse things happen at sea ...'
'True, O King ...!'
'Chance'd be a fine thing ...'
'*Sic Transit* Gloria Swanson ...'

'Read any good books lately ...?'
'Yes, and I've got medals to prove it ...'
'Well, that's my story and I'm sticking to it ...'
'What's that got to do with the price of carrots?'

and:

'Yes, what a lot of weather there's been lately ...'

Care should be taken in using three such gluesome phrases, lest they cause trouble. I'm thinking of:

'Well, he would, wouldn't he?'
'Ah, well, keeps them off the streets ...'

and:

'It takes one to know one ...'

I was present at a most embarrassing occasion when a speaker inadvertently used the third of these instead of the first. She was being introduced to Mr G——— B———, a well-known writer and 'personality'. The introducer said: 'I'd like you to meet Mr G——— B———, who has written a book called *Great Sexual Disasters*.'

However, I can rccommcnd without qualification the casual flinging in of the following phrases. They will grace any conversation:

'Oh really? Nobody never tells me nuffink ...'
'There's a lot of it about ...'
'Something in the water, I expect ...'
'Water under the bridge, old chap ...'
'... Or I'm a Dutchman ...'
'Not by a long chalk ...'
'But does the end justify the means?'
'How now, brown cow?'
'What can I say?!'
'No names, no pack drill ...'
'Some of my best friends are ...'
'It seemed like a good idea at the time ...'
'Between these four walls ...'
'Between you, me, and the bed-post ...'
'Out of the frying pan and into the fire ...'

Don't neglect the useful formula:

'Every ——, gets the —— it deserves'

– as in, 'Every country gets the politician/television/

weather/ice-skaters it deserves.' 'Every book gets the publisher it deserves'. And so on.

Special attention should be drawn to one invaluable conversation-filler:

'I tried it once, but I didn't like it …'

An ace user of this turn of phrase was the late publishing giant, Sir Stanley Unwin (not to be confused with the comedian.) At some function or other, he was dining with a visiting foreign publisher who offered him a cigarette. Sir Stanley sharply rejected the offer, saying, 'I tried it once, but I didn't like it …' Later, towards the end of the meal, the foreign publisher suggested some brandy. Again, Sir Stanley rejected the offer, saying, 'Tried it once, didn't like it …'

Next day, the two of them happened to bump into Sir Stanley's son, Rayner. Sir Stanley made to introduce the boy, but, quick as a flash, the foreigner quipped, 'Your *only* son, I take it?'

Now this wasn't really fair on Sir Stanley, not letting him get it out for a third time, and, what's more, it wasn't factually accurate. But I think he'd done pretty well with his phrase to date and I think he deserves a round of applause. (APPLAUSE).

I have had a special request for conversation-fillers that can safely be employed when chatting with the Archbishop of Canterbury. 'No problema!', as his Holiness Pope Paul VI used to say. What follows has already been tried out by me in intercourse with His Grace at a special prayer meeting at Lambeth Palace:

'Great minds think alike …'

'Don't get your knickers in a twist …!'

'Confucius, he say …'

'Not many people know that, Your Grace …'

'Makes you think, don't it …?'

'Listen, darling, they're playing our tune …'

When he happens to mention that he is going to be officiating at a forthcoming wedding at St Paul's Cathedral, throw in:

'Anyone we know …?'

'Yes, we had one but the wheel came off ...'

'Keep taking the tablets ...'

There is no need to add 'Your Grace' at the end of each sentence.

Finally, may I recommend a conversation-filler *par excellence*, as in:

'I'll certainly do it for you, **D.V.W.P.X.Y.Z.**'

This, of course, means '*Deo volo*' and 'weather permitting' (with 'X.Y.Z.' thrown in for good measure.)

Conversation Tennis

By this I mean certain exchanges that you should practise with a partner and then perform whenever you find a suitable opportunity.

For example, PLAYER 1 asks:

'What day is it?'

and PLAYER 2 replies:

'Tuesday – **all day!'**

Another example:

PLAYER 1: 'What's the time?'

PLAYER 2: 'Half-past nine.'

and PLAYER 1 chimes in with:

'Hang your knickers on the line!'

And here is one you can use to fill up those long, boring railway journeys:

PLAYER 1: 'Is this Wembley?'

PLAYER 2: 'No, it's Thursday.'

PLAYER 3: **'So am I. Let's have a drink!'**

I am printing both sides of some more witty and sparkling exchanges below. If you think you know the answers, why not cover over the right-hand column with a piece of card and test your skill? Here goes:

PLAYER 1	
'How are you?'	**'All the better for seeing you!'**
'Do you like Kipling?'	**'I don't know, I've never kippled.'**
''Ere we go then ...'	**'As the earwig said as it fell down the stairs.'**
'I've lost my virginity.'	**'Have you kept the box it came in?'**
'Do you believe in sex before marriage?'	**'Not if it delays the ceremony.'**
'Who told you that?'	**'A little bird told me.'**
'Does it hurt?'	**'Only when I laugh.'**
'Have you got the time?'	**'I've got the time if you've got the inclination.'**
'Is the "t" in "buffet" silent?'	**'Not the way I drink it.'**
'I've got a touch of the dreaded nadgers.'	**'There's a lot of it about.'**
'How do porcupines make love?'	**'Very carefully.'**
'How do armadillos make love?'	**'With difficulty.'**
'How do human beings make love?'	**'Ask a silly question, get a silly answer.'**

Encyclopedia Britannica

When completely stumped for something to say, here is a useful tip: recite what it says on the spines of your set of the *Encylopedia Britannica.* Think about what it says there and you will find, in no time at all, that you have acquired fascinating subjects for conversation and discussion.

Here goes. First of all, look at the Micropedia:

'A – Bib
'Bibai – Coleman
'Colemani – Exclusi
'Excom – Hermosil
'Hermoup – Lally
'Lalo – Montpar
'Montpel – Piranesi
'Piranha – Scurfy
'Scurlock – Tirah
'Tirane – Zywny.'

There! Absolute magic. Now, weave a story round these fascinating characters. 'Lalo Montpar' is clearly a somewhat mysterious jazz musician (if not an anagram) who comes up against the frightening underworld figure of 'Piranha Scurfy'. Just take it from there …

If you find this too difficult, go for Macropedia spines and make connections between them, e.g.:

Taylor + Utah
Sonar + Tax Law
Peking + Probability
Conifer + Ear Diseases

Surely 'Conifer Ear Diseases' is a subject on which you have something to say?

Exclamations

Nothing brightens up a conversation more quickly than a well-placed exclamation. Obvious examples would include:

'Great balls of fire!'
'Great Scott!'
'*Gesundheit*!' (also useful after a sneeze – it's German for 'health')
'Gentleman, lift the seat!' (this is also a toast)
'Laugh? I could have died!'
'Oh, my sainted aunt!'
'Oh, my giddy aunt!'
'Eat your heart out!'
'Damn clever these Chinese!'

'The mind boggles!'
'Scout's honour!'
'Do you think I can shit miracles?'
'Never a dull moment, eh?'
'Excuse me for breathing!'
'I should coco!'
'Sorry I spoke!'

Men should always exclaim:

'Women and children first!'

Sloane Rangers should always exclaim:

'V.G.!'

and:

'Absoballylutely!'

This last one reminds me of the time when I was at the theatre on the very night that the Lord Chamberlain's powers of stage censorship were abolished in 1969 – a momentous moment, and one that was brought home to us by that excellent actor Mr Paul Scofield (isn't it time he got a knighthood, by the way?) exclaiming:

'Fanfuckingtastic!'

(The play was John Osborne's *The Hotel in Amsterdam*, incidentally.) I remember the occasion well. I think it showed remarkable restraint not to go the whole hog and exclaim:

'Oh, how fanfuckingbloodyabsolutelytastic!'

Sensitive souls may care to use the more restrained:

'My flabber has never been more gasted.'

(See also SWEARING).

Family Jokes

Most of these are pretty impenetrable to outsiders. I might just pass on two that ruled in my own nest. If ever anything unaccountable happened about the house – something went missing or went wrong – then the explanation was:

'Oh, it's Ivor ...'

A very useful person to have about the house.

Another, which sprang from an incident in my childhood

when I had encouraged the family to walk through a field with a bull in it, was:

'Don't go through a field with a bull in it!'

– addressed to someone who was tempting providence.

You may use these or manufacture your own.

Foreign Tags, Casually Tossed In

Any conversation can be enlivened immeasurably by the casual tossing in of a French or Latin tag. This procedure lends tone and dignity to intercourse. In no particular order, here are the top ten such phrases:

1) ***'Chacun à son gout.'*** ('It's all the port he drinks that does it')
2) ***'Facilis descensus averni.'*** ('It's quicker by Tube')
3) ***'Où sont les neiges d'antan?'*** ('Have you seen my undies anywhere?')
4) ***'Eheu fugaces.'*** ('Poo, what a stink!')
5) ***'Merde'*** ('Oh dear')
6) ***'Tout passe, tout casse, tout lasse.'*** ('Nothing lasts very long these days, does it?')
7) ***'Cherchez la femme.'*** ('Have you seen my wife anywhere?')
8) ***'Revenons à nos moutons.'*** ('Would you like some of yesterday's lamb?')
9) ***'L'amour – toujours l'amour.'*** ('He's always at it')
10) ***'Quel fromage!'*** ('What a pity!)

Opening Gambits

The most difficult part of any conversation comes at the very beginning. How to get started? Some people, of course, never do. They can sit next to someone at a dinner party or in a railway carriage, inwardly twisting and writhing, but incapable of squeezing out the few words needed to set the conversational ball rolling.

I will now supply you with those few words.

I would not recommend the approach once used, long ago, by the actor, Mr Kenneth Williams, to me. He asked:

'Are you getting your fucks all right?'

I believe I assented and a conversation did indeed begin which has continued almost uninterrupted ever since, though I am still waiting to get a word in. On the whole, however, I would not recommend this approach. Equally to be avoided are such openers as:

'Did you get your rocks off last night?'

and:

'Which way do you dress?'

It is probably better to try something less controversial, viz.:

'Are you happy in your work?'

or:

'Have you stopped beating your wife?'

Expert conversationalists swear by the somewhat more oblique:

'There are fairies at the bottom of my garden – how about yours?'

and:

'The rain in Spain falls mainly on the plain'

and the formula:

'I've never been one for ——. I'm more of a —— man myself'

– as in, 'I've never been one for Thatcher. I'm more of a tit man myself.'

It is suggested, in certain circles, that you should always begin dinner party conversations by asking:

'How's the book coming along?'

because everyone is either writing a book or intending to.

However, be careful not to try this approach in the company of the noted satirist, Mr Peter Cook. Attempting to start up a conversation, he asked someone, 'What are you doing at the moment?' The person replied, 'Writing a book.' And Peter countered with: 'Neither am I.'

Proverbs

I do not recommend the use of proverbs in conversations of quality. They have a way of lowering the tone of the whole proceedings. What I do recommend is the insertion of resonant-sounding proverbial sayings of your own devising, even if their meaning is somewhat hard to fathom.

Winston Fletcher, advertising guru, deals with this sphere in his seminal work, *Meetings, Meetings*. He quotes a past master of the genre, Jeremy Bullmore, chairman of J. Walter Thompson, as saying:

'Somebody has to bury the undertaker ...'

'It may not be the man who saws the logs who needs the fire.'

Freddie Tarrant, a head-hunter, chimes in with:

'After all, a door has to be closed before it can be opened.'

And Joseph Berkman, a restaurant owner, produces the superb:

'As we always say in Austria, those who have butter on their heads don't walk in the sun.'

(Note the devastating use of 'As we always say in ...')

Studying the above examples will enable you to see the very simple mechanism that lies behind these useful conversation-enhancers. In time, you will feel confident enough to manufacture your own:

'Even a short leg reaches the ground'

(Congratulations to Dr Walter Heydecker who originated this one.)

'There are more ways to skin a cat than stuffing it with strawberries.'

'Every time a sheep bleats it loses a nibble.'

If you feel at all apprehensive, begin by rubbing together a few standard proverbs and quotations and observing the results:

'You can lead a horse to the water, but you can't force rhubarb.'

'When one door closes, another door closes.'

' "Curiouser and curiouser", said the cat.'

'Too many cooks make a white.'
'Two blacks don't make a wrong.'
'Marry in haste; try, try again.'
'A bird in the hand spoils the broth.'

You will enjoy this life-enhancing experience.

On no account should you pretend that your made-up proverbs are authentic. Messrs Auden and Isherwood came up with:

'Pissing in his shoes keeps no man warm for long'

and:

'Every man likes the smell of his own farts.'

They called these 'Icelandic proverbs'. A likely story.

Quotations

Now who was it who said, 'He used quotations as a drunk does a lamp-post – more for support than illumination'? I can't for the life of me remember. That's the trouble with quotations, far too much trouble. Indeed, this author firmly believes that you should never use quotations in conversation. He has studiously avoided them all his life. In addition, he once said, 'One of my ambitions is never to say anything quotable.' Unfortunately, this was quoted in a magazine called *Honey*, of all places.

There are, nevertheless, one or two *allusions* that it does no harm to drop into your talk:

'It is closing time in the gardens of the West ...'

(this is something once said by Cyril Connolly, but you should never attribute quotations. After all what is a quotation but plagiarism *with* acknowledgement – and we don't want any of that, do we?)

'Remember, without eternal vigilance, it could happen here ...'

'*C'est magnifique mais ce n'est pas la gare.*'

'The situation in Germany is serious but not hopeless. The situation in Austria is hopeless, but not serious ...'

'I didn't promise you a rose garden ...'

'The trivial round, the common task, A cup of tea is all we ask ...'

It is also in order to make use of Chinese sayings, like the curse:

'May you live in interesting times!'

or, for that matter, Irish sayings, like the curse:

'May your wife eat biscuits in bed!'

as there is no way of checking their authenticity.

The general aim is to say something which would get you a 'Hear, hear!' in the House of Commons. These examples should set you off in the right direction.

Saying Things You Want Overheard

A whole industry has unfortunately grown up around people eavesdropping on conversations, quoting remarks out of context, and sending them in to radio programmes and even putting them into little books. Should you feel the need to scuttle this procedure, or render it valueless, you should go around making absurd, plonking remarks, especially on the tops of buses. To achieve the desired effect, it helps if you are two little old ladies.

Say things like:

'I've felt so much better since I had my back passage painted green'

or:

'It was one of those things you die of whether you've got it or not.'

Take care. There is nothing worse than a wrongly-constructed eavesdropping and you will surely be held up to ridicule and contempt if you fail.

Weather

Weather is the one topic of conversation on which the British need absolutely no instruction. It is a gift they receive at birth. Even before they can walk, they crawl around saying things like:

'My, it's cold enough to freeze the balls off a brass monkey'

'Winter draws on!'

and:

'It said on the weather forecast ...'

So, no further instruction will be provided.

I once heard an American from the West coast ask one from the East coast the question, 'Do you have weather?' On the whole, however, foreigners don't have weather, so, quite rightly, they don't need to talk about it.

Wise Saws

According to Shakespeare, you will remember, a 'wise saw', like a 'modern instance', is the sort of thing that mature persons in the fifth age of man like to fling into their conversation at appropriate moments. Rather like CONVERSATION GLUE (*q.v.*), Wise Saws keep the talk bubbling along. They often have the function of a grunt of agreement; at other times they give added weight and purpose to your discourse, however randomly selected. From the many to hand, I have selected the following excellent miniature homilies. It would be best for you to choose no more than half a dozen ancient pieces of wisdom that you particularly like and try to hand them on as often as you can through conversation. They are often best preceded by the word, 'Aye, ...'

1. **'It takes two to tango ..."**
2. **'It's more by good luck than good management ...'**
3. **'If you keep digging, you'll end up in Australia ...'**
4. **'They don't make 'em like that any more ...'**
   (but see also SHOWBIZ FOLK.)
5. **'God helps those who help themselves ...'**
6. **'The higher they are, the harder they fall ...'**
7. **'There are lies, damned lies and statistics ...'**
8. **'Where there's muck, there's brass ...'**
9. **'There's nowt so queer as folk ...'**
   (the addition of 'as they say in Yorkshire' is entirely up to the individual speaker.)
10. **'Give him an inch and he'll take a yard ...'**
11. **'All's fair in love and war ...'**
12. **'Never judge a cigar by the label on the box ...'**

13. (To a small person:) **'They don't make diamonds as big as bricks ...'**
14. **'Truth is stranger than fiction ...'**
15. **'Always be nice to people on your way up because you'll meet them again on your way down ...'**
16. **'Lightning never strikes twice in the same place ...'**
17. **'Never look a gift horse in the mouth ...'**
18. **'You can't put the toothpaste back in the tube ...'**
19. **'Believe nothing that you hear and only half of what you see ...'**
20. **'Horses sweat, men perspire, but ladies merely glow ...'**
21. **'The proof of the pudding is in the eating ...'**
22. **'All men are equal, but some are more equal than others ...'**
23. **'The nearer the bone, the sweeter the meat ...'**
24. **'In the kindgom of the blind, the one-eyed man is king ...'**
25. **'You can't make an omelette without breaking eggs ...'**
26. **'Every dog has its day and every cat its night out ...'**
27. **'We can't go home, 'cos you can't eat sun ...'**
    (Commonwealth immigrants, for the use of)
28. **'The darkest hour comes just before the dawn ...'**
29. **'It'll only end in tears ...'**

Go forth, and speak them!

Wit

There have been many definitions of wit, none of which I can recall off-hand, so we are forced to rely on the best rule of thumb of all, namely, that we know wit when we encounter it.

We can but wilt in admiration at the man who walks into a bar and says:

'Give me a crocodile sandwich – and make it snappy!'

It seems so right for the situation. Yet wit comes in different forms. My maternal grandfather was a very witty man and his jokes have been handed down and around with loving care. Driving past a cemetery, he would say: 'That's where they bury the deaf and dumb.' When we expressed admiration at his knowledge of the locality and asked how he knew, he would reply:

'All dead people are deaf and dumb!'

You can see how he acquired his reputation.

I can but recall some of the other genuinely witty people I have met in my life. Take Geoffrey, my dresser at Yorkshire Television, for instance. I was unpacking some rather expensive Jaeger shirts from my suitcase not so long ago and, quick as a flash, Geoffrey came out with:

'I used to go shoplifting – but those shops are too heavy!'

I wrote it down straight away to be sure I wouldn't forget it.

Then there was one of my schoolmasters – a French teacher to be exact. He had a very witty remark which we heard quite often:

'In Paris there are only two types of pedestrian – the quick and the dead!'

Gallic wit, you see.

Augustus Pettifer, a market gardener, combined wit with the scatological in interesting proportions. He would say:

'The cat crept into the crypt, had a crap, and crept out again!'

If encouraged by me, and plied with his favourite brew, he would allow a glimpse of his other one:

'The Pope popped up to the poop, had a peep, and popped down again!'

This, however, was thought to be rather in advance of its time, in some quarters. It was Augustus, too, who would frequently declare:

'Far from being disgruntled, I'm positively gruntled!'

But then, he was that sort of chap. We all miss him now.

Talking of wits of yesteryear, as we have been, I think it was Oscar Wilde who must have formulated four priceless and much-quoted examples. See if you can match the feedlines to the punchlines:

FEEDLINE

1) 'My ancestor lost a leg at Waterloo.'
2) 'Who was that lady I saw you with last night?'

3) 'How long will the next bus be?'
4) 'Do you know your wife's unfaithful?'

PUNCHLINE
a) 'Same length as this.'
b) 'Good gracious! Which platform?'
c) 'That was no lady – that was my wife!'
d) 'No, but hum it and I'll pick up the tune.'

ANSWERS
1) + a
2) + b
3) + c
4) + d

Wilde's modern equal, in so many ways, is Orson Welles, the American personality. Well-fortified with sherry he is an incomparable master of the witty one-liner. Some of the pearls I have been privileged to hear tumbling from his lips include:

'If a thing is worth doing, it's worth doing badly.'
'Hell hath no fury like a woman's corns.'
'Faith can move mountains – she's a big girl.'
'They call me "Fatso" for short – but not for long!'

When asked to explain how his surname was pronounced, he wittily replied:

'The "p" is silent – as in swimming.'

Though perhaps I'm mistaking Orson for someone else.

(I need hardly add that 'Knock-Knock' jokes of the type:
'Knock-knock.'
'Who's there?'
'Bell.'
'Bell who?'
'Bell's broken'
– should be rigorously excluded from this category.

The same is true of Elephant jokes, viz.:
'Why don't Elephants like Penguins?'
'I don't know, why don't Elephants like Penguins?'
'Because they can't be bothered to take the wrappers off.'
As I say, you'll know wit when you hear it.)

Part 4
What To Say When ...

Answering the Telephone

People find it very amusing if you answer the phone and say:

'Hello? Chinese laundry!'

or:

'Battersea Dogs Home?!'

or simply:

'Yes, sir, no, sir, three bags full, sir!'

before replacing the receiver.

On the other hand, many people have answering machines these days and leave them permanently switched on to avoid having to deal with anyone directly. There is some debate as to whether or not you should reveal your name on the answering machine message. Some people simply give their number. This is said to foil burglars. However, by not giving your name you can find yourself receiving messages not intended for you. Some years ago I played back the messages on my 'anonymous' answering machine and found one, delivered in a broad Italian accent, asking for a delivery of 'two-a dozen-a gallons-a strawberry ice-a cream-a.' Alas, whoever it was never got them.

Be warned, it is best not to possess an answering machine if there is any likelihood of your being rung up by clergymen. It is like a red rag to a bull, I can tell you. Give them a short burst of tone and they are on for hours. No, the best message to put on your machine is:

'So-and-so is **unable to come to the phone at the moment.'**

This suggests clearly that you are either stuck in the loo, making ecstatic love, or on holiday six thousand miles away.

The best message to leave on other people's answering machines is:

'Hello, it's me!'

(Don't leave your name and number, in case of burglars.)

Should you suspect that someone is listening in to your conversation on a crossed line or phone-tap, you should say things like:

(*In a very boring voice*) **'All right, I'll see you on Sunday then. And don't forget to bring your rompers ...'**

That should give them something to think about.

While on the subject of telephones, people of great dignity should not be afraid of showing affection over the instrument. I was once with a distinguished stockbroker when he rang his wife to tell her which train he was going to catch home to Gerrard's Cross, or wherever he lived. Before he rang off, he intoned with great seriousness, the little rhyme:

'See you soon,
Oh baboon.'

Being Offered A Drink

First of all, in the best circles, when offering sugar for tea or coffee, people ask:

'Sugar? Or are you sweet enough as you are?'

When declining a second cup, they say:

'No, thank you, I'm a one-cup man myself.'

So, taking it on from there, persons offering you alcoholic drinks should make use of one of the following expressions:

'Shall we splice the main brace?'

'The sun's below the yard-arm, so, time for a little something?'

'Hair of the dog that bit you?'

'This'll put lead in your pencil/hairs on your chest!'

When topping up your glass the person should say:

'Let me replenish your glass'

'May I refresh your glass?'

'Another cup of tea, vicar?'

If you are on the receiving end, you should greet these offers thus:

'Well, perhaps just a small one …'
'A dray wait wane for me, please …'
'Just a drop to be sociable!'
(mandatory if you are a maiden aunt)
'Another little drink wouldn't do us any harm!'
'Another little drinkie? Why not?!'
'Just for medicinal purposes, of course!'
(accent on third syllable of 'medicinal')

Should you be declining drinks and refills, note these expressions:

'Oh, no thank you. I like it, but it doesn't like me!' (Cf. Dr Swift's example in the Preface)
'No, thank you, I've had enough liquid refreshment.'

Raising your glass, say:

'Skol!'
'Here's mud in your eye!'
'Bottoms up!'
'Up yours!'

or words to that effect.

When stopped by the police on the way home, you should say:

'Good consternoon, affable'

or:

'I'm not under the affluence of incohol.'

Your wife should tell the policeman:

'Take no notice, officer, he's always like this when he's had a few.'

Celebrating Your Wedding Anniversary

You should send your spouse a card saying something to this effect:

'Happy tenth wedding anniversary, darling. Thank you for seven wonderful years.'

See how well that goes down.

Chatting Up

Vigorous research and thorough revision has been devoted to this subject since my own technique was clearly falling behind the times and failing to come up with the goods.

For example, a long, long time ago in a galaxy far, far away, I once made an attempt upon the person of Clare Francis, then a diminutive teenager. She later became, of course, an intrepid transatlantic helmsperson and born-again novelist. (Incidentally, I hope we're both grown-up enough and sufficiently famous for it to be OK for me to reveal this sort of mild anecdote, historic in its way.) It being then the early 1960s, I tentatively ventured the traditional line:

'And what does your father do?'

Yes, I know, very funny and all that now, but in those days it really was the sort of thing you asked girls when you were trying to break the ice. She replied, 'Oh ... he's a sort of electrician.'

I thought this a bit rum at the time and it was only several years later that I discovered he'd been Chairman of the London Electricity Board, or some such.

So, quite clearly, you'd best avoid anything like that.

Similarly, 'I could get you into pictures' is positively OUT. Without question. The contemporary version is:

'I could get you a part in a video'

or, more practically:

'I could help get you an Equity card.'

It is unwise to use the familiar, 'What is it, darling? Don't you recognize me with my clothes on?' This has been modified to suit the occasion when you bump into a Page 3 Girl propping up the bar. You should say to her:

'Sorry, I didn't recognize you with your clothes on.'

She can then say:

'With yours on, you don't look the same either.'

This passes for wit in those circles.

We are aiming at something a little more couth than:

''Ello, darlin', on yer own?'

or:

'Getting enough?'

However:

'Haven't we met somewhere before?'

is still as good as ever for breaking the ice.

A contemporary effective list of tried and tested chat-up lines would read as follows:

1. **'Excuse me, but haven't I seen you on TV?'** (NOT 'Excuse me, but aren't you Miss World?')
2. **'Does your suntan go all over?'**
3. **'Does your mother know you're out?'**
4. **'How do you like your eggs done for breakfast?'** (a bit bold this, but it may be worth trying.)
5. **'How did you get into those jeans?'**
6. **'You've got the most kissable lips in London?'** (I heard this used at the next table to me in a restaurant very recently. They weren't, but it seemed to have the desired effect. Which just goes to show.)
7. **'Are you a Virgo?'**
8. **'Hello, twinkle-tits!'** (be terribly careful with this one, although it's a personal favourite of mine.)
9. **'You're the sort of woman my mother warned me about and I never thought I'd have the luck to meet.'**
10. **'Did anyone ever tell you that you're beautiful?'**
11. **'My god, you're ugly!'** (NB. This is ironic.)
12. **'What a great pair of … eyes you've got.'**
13. (*At parties:*) **'Are you as bored as I am?'**
14. **'Here's looking at you, kid!'**
15. **'Do you play cards?'**
    'Yes …'
16. **'Well, if you play your cards right you can take me out tonight!'**

(And, if you want to skip the first stage and get right on with seduction:)

17. **'Lie down – I think I love you!'**
18. **'Fancy a little horizontal jogging?'**
19. **'Where do you get your oats?'**
20. **'I could go for you in a big way …'**
21. **'What's your pleasure?'**

22. **'Little girls don't want to be getting on their bikes at this time of night, do they?'**
    (A seventy-two-year-old former BBC newsreader speaks highly of this one.)
23. **'I'd like to have Biblical knowledge of you ...'**
24. **'If I could think of a good chat-up line, I'd use it on you ...!'**
25. **'I've only got six months to live ...'**
26. **'I suppose a fuck's out of the question?'**
27. **'Are you keeping it for the worms?'**
28. **'We'll get married just as soon as the divorce comes through ...'**

If you are a married man but wish to express your appreciation of some untouchable vision of delight, you cannot do better than utter the excellent American saying:

29. **'I love my wife – but, oh, you kid!'**

What a charming moist feel that has to it!

Unfortunately, I am at a loss to suggest what expressions women should use when chatting up men, if indeed they do. I suppose they could try:

30. **'And what does your mother do?'**

(For the other side to such 'conversations' see REJECTING AMOROUS ADVANCES.)

Consoling People

In general, if a person is down in the dumps, or, if he is a swan-upper, actually *has* down in the dumps, there is not a great deal you can say to lift his spirits. Try asking, however:

'What's the worst that could happen?'

or pass on Dr Johnson's admirable advice:

'Consider, sir, how it will appear twelve months hence.'

After a person has shuffled off this mortal coil, gone to the Bourne from which no Hollingsworth returns, joined the Vale of Tears, kicked the bucket and handed in his dinner-pail, family and friends should console themselves with these fine thoughts:

'Well, he had a good innings …'
'He died as he would have wished … in bed.'
'It was a relief really …'
'Better not to have dragged it out …'
'His death must not have been in vain.'
'He did not die in vain.'
'It couldn't have happened to a nicer chap.'
'It shouldn't happen to a dog.'

When someone announces, 'I've got some sad news for you,' jump in first with:

'No, don't tell me who, allow me to guess!'

Dining At Buckingham Palace

If there are two things that people have more nightmares about than any other they are 1) what to say at table, and 2) what to say when meeting the Queen. So, as a further service to mankind, I have decided to amalgamate these two fears and set your minds at rest about … what to say at table when dining at Buckingham Palace with HM the Queen.

A lot of nonsense is talked about such occasions: that you should only speak when you are spoken to, and such like. But my advice is quite the opposite. The Queen is a very small person, a bit on the shy side, and needs all the encouragement you can give her.

Greet Her with a slap on the back and a cheery:

'I hope you are keeping your pecker up, Your Majesty!'

You can then drop the 'Your Majesty', but continue to throw in the occasional 'ma'am', as in:

'Bloody hell, ma'am, is that the time?'

There is a very good precedent for this. When a burglar penetrated the Queen's bedroom in 1982, Elizabeth Andrews, her chambermaid, exclaimed impeccably: 'Bloody hell, ma'am, what's he doing in here?'

As soon as you arrive, let Her know how much you are looking forward to the meal. Exclaim:

'I could eat a horse!'

or:

'I could eat the hind leg off a donkey!'

or:

'My belly-button's playing hell with my backbone!'

She will probably have a footman press a dry Amontillado into your hand. Use it to gesture at her priceless oil paintings, whilst remarking about a particular portrait:

'I haven't seen her for yonks!'

or, of a still life:

'That's the hottest thing since sliced bread.'

When the Queen asks if you, too, collect paintings, reply:

'D'you think I'm made of money, or something?'

'Money doesn't grow on trees, you know!'

When the Chief Butler of England announces that the meal is served, say:

'Come and get it!'

or:

'Come on, we'll go through this like a dose of salts.'

Take care when eating the soup. Say to the footman who is pouring it out for you:

'Just a *soupçon*(!) ... in case it doesn't agree with me!'

Or, if it is one of those informal affairs that the Queen sometimes gives, seize the tureen and inquire:

'Now, which of us is going to be mother?'

– and hope that Queen Elizabeth the Queen Mother doesn't take offence.

Should service be slow, clap your hands and say:

'Come on, chop, chop!'

Tucking in to the nosh, affirm loudly:

'That's the stuff to give the troops!'

and:

'My compliments to the chef!'

Should someone ask, 'Has anyone seen the salt?' – say:

'Finders, keepers!'

Should you get offered second helpings, the correct thing to say, wiping your mouth, is:

'No, thank you, **I've had an excellent sufficiency!**'

You may, however, relent under pressure and say:

'Well, all right, **if you insist!**'

If *you* are doing the offering of second helpings, say:

'Any more for any more?'

Should there be a single portion of anything left, press it on Her Majesty with the words:

'A thousand a year?'

(Don't ask me why this belief should have taken root, but we always say it in our house, so why not at Buckingham Palace?)

Useful things to say to people seated to right and left of you during the meal, include:

'Elbows off the table, dear.'

'Don't talk with your mouth full!'

'Your eyes are bigger than your stomach!'

'Eat your greens!'

'Yes, Princess Anne told me herself. **I got it straight from the horse's mouth …'**

'Did you know, Mr Gladstone masturbated thirty-two times before swallowing?'

'I think this is kind of immoral when people are starving in India …'

'Stop looking at your watch!'

Should you enjoy the meat course particularly, remark loudly:

'One of the corgis not missing, is it?'

Or, if it is the fish you like, mention:

'The piece of cod that passeth all understanding.'

Should anything not agree with you, remark philosophically:

'Ah, well, it'll all come out in the wash!'

Over coffee and brandy, clap your hands together, give a wink to Prince Philip, and cry:

'Bring on the dancing girls!'

Should this first visit to Buck House go down well, you will almost certainly get invited back – perhaps to one of those special luncheon parties that the Queen gives, you know, the ones where the guests include a well-known thriller writer, a professor of paleontology, a trade union leader, an Irish chat show host and you. Being a touch more familiar with Her Majesty, you should say:

'I didn't recognize you without your crown on!'

– that always goes down well. You may care to engage her in more profound conversation this time, too. Begin:

'Come the revolution ...'

or:

'When I'm dictator ...'

– not forgetting to add the 'ma'am', of course.

When you knock over the gravy boat, say:

'Whoops! Just as well we're not at Buckingham Palace, eh?'

or, when Prince Philip knocks over the gravy boat:

'You can't take him anywhere, can you?'

When offered a cigar after the meal, decline with:

'No, thank you, I only smoke on special occasions!'

– He always hoots at that one, too.

Finally, you should say to the assembled company:

'You may get down now!'

It will have been a once in a lifetime experience for you, in more ways than one.

Doing A Thomas à Becket

Say blithely to your private army:

'Will no man rid me of this man?'

– as Henry II said concerning Thomas à Becket (and look what happened there.) Alternatively:

'Who will rid me of this turbulent priest?'

NB: Accept absolutely no responsibility for the content and outcome of these remarks.

Enjoying Christmas

These are the traditional yuletide things to say:

'It's not what it was, is it?'
'It's for the children, really, of course ...'
'I'll be glad when it's all over.'
'When is everybody arriving?'

'When is everybody leaving?'
'What time is lunch going to be?'
'Never again!'

Round about midnight on Christmas Eve, fathers should say in a loud voice (as mine did once):

'Have you filled Nigel's stocking yet?'

After Christmas, you must always ask people:

'Did you have a good Christmas?'

– and they'll probably tell you.

Explaining The Facts Of Life

When discussing the facts of life with their offspring, parents should not make the usual mess of it if they make use of the following instructions. Fathers should puff at a pipe. They should declare:

'Not everyone has the same standards as your mother and I'

and warn their sons about:

'Odd chaps'

whom they might encounter at the university.

Should they ever get round to naming the male private part, they should call it:

'Your scampi.'

Mothers should point out that:

'Sex was only designed to be consumed in marriage.'

On the subject of declining horizontal pleasure, daughters should be given the excellent and original advice:

'Cross your legs, dear, and take a pickled onion.'

Finding Your Hostess Naked In The Bath

I understand this to have happened and that the unfortunate intruder only managed to mumble the inappropriate words: 'My, you do look well!' Clearly, this was gauche in the extreme after a fox's pass of such magnitude. He hardly came up smelling of violets. Nor, I imagine, did she.

So, I decided to consult Douglas Sutherland, author of the *English Gentlemen* series of books, who advised:

'I beg your pardon, *sir*!'

This sounded much better, and I subsequently found confirmation that it was the correct response when reading a 1932 novel, *Charming Manners* by John Michaelhouse. In the story, a group of Oxford undergraduates happen upon half a dozen naked nymphs dancing in the sunlight on the banks of the River Cherwell. 'We all collapsed in the punt at once, there being no chance of saying "Sorry, gentlemen," in the approved style.'

So that seems to be it, then.

Giving A Vote Of Thanks

Quite the nicest thing I ever had said to me after a speech on the subject of quotations (see QUOTATIONS) was, 'When we were at school I could never remember which way up to put quotation marks – whether to put 66 or 99. Well, today, all the quotations marks have been the right way up.' But this is exceeding necessity. Settle instead for:

'Thank you for sparing us a little of your valuable time.'

'By the time of your next visit, I hope you'll be in *Who's Who* so that we know what to expect.'

'A good time has been had by all.'

Going Backstage

Further to the excellent advice on visiting thespians after the show contained in *The Joy of Clichés*, let me add just two more very useful phrases. They have the virtue of not committing you too deeply in your praise for the performance you have just witnessed. They are:

1) **'It was so *you*!'**

and:

2) **'What can I say ...?'**

Be careful, however, when throwing in:

'How wise of you not to attempt a French accent!'
as this may be misconstrued.

Going Through The Door With Someone

Only a very limited choice here, I'm afraid. It's either:
1) **'Age before beauty ...'**
or:
2) **'After you, Claude ... no, after you, Cecil!'**
But these are so good, it would be hard to better them.

Going To The Lavatory

Few human activities demand more care when being talked about than the whole business of going to the loo. At school we are told to ask:
'Please, miss, may I leave the room?'
or:
'Please, sir, may I be excused?'
From then on we are completely inhibited about it.

So, take a leaf out of my Uncle Tom's book. He was a pilot in the Battle of Britain, and always states calmly, but authoritatively:
'I'm just going to make a telephone call to Hitler.'
Should he need to make a return visit, he will remark quietly, but firmly:
'Here comes the reply ...'
Other original ways of overcoming the embarrassment are to say:
'I'm just going to powder my nose ...'
'I'm just going to wash my hands ...'
'Where's the cloakroom?'
'I have to answer the call of nature.'
'I've got to shake hands with the wife's best friend.'
The more adventurous may feel like attempting:
'When you've gotta go, you've gotta go.'
Businessmen's secretaries should not reveal where their

bosses are momentarily holed up, but merely say:

'He's in the little boy's room.'

Another two things to say when you want to go to the loo Down Under:

'I'm just going to point Percy at the porcelain'

and:

'I'm going to the biscuit factory.'*

Greeting Newly-Weds

Say to the bride:

'May I be the first to call you Mrs ——?'

and, if there is to be a skiing honeymoon:

'Take care on the nursery slopes!'

To the groom, regarding the honeymoon, inquire:

'Are you going all the way tonight?'

Guesting On Chat Shows

You are poised at the top of the stairs, the host says, 'Will you welcome ...', the band strikes up, and you are on.

Nowadays, there are so many radio and TV chat shows that they are bound to get around to inviting you on to one soon. An appearance on a nationally-aired chat show is the logical outcome of a careful study of the contents of this book. It can be a bit of an ordeal for the newcomer, however, hence the following tips.

How it all goes rather depends on the host. Some hosts glaze over as soon as you start talking, very distracting. Some rely very heavily on idiot boards, large bits of cardboard held up just out of camera range with their questions on. Mike Douglas, the great American chat show person, is supposed to have misread a question from one of his idiot boards on one occasion. He was meant to ask Kirk

* There was a make of biscuit in South Australia called Menz.

Douglas (no relation), 'IS THIS AN EPIC MOVIE YOU'RE STARRING IN?' Unfortunately, he asked Kirk:

'Is this an Eric movie you're starring in?'

Something similar happened to me when I was guesting on a chat show in Australia. The host was doing the whole thing from idiot boards. He had two questions like 'ARE YOU GOING ON TO NEW ZEALAND?' and 'IS THE PRINCESS OF WALES GOING TO HAVE A BABY?' Unfortunately, he ran the two questions together and they came out as:

'Are you going to New Zealand to have a baby?'

When I found this a little hard to answer, I noticed that familiar glazed look coming over him and it was suddenly time for another commercial break, while I disappeared through a hole in the floor.

There is also a technique, much practised, whereby you don't actually get to meet the host until you shake hands with him on screen. A researcher comes to interview you instead, and thus you have to get across to the host what you want to say in advance through an intermediary. One of Michael Parkinson's researchers once described this process as 'Holding Mike's coat while he makes love'.

Whenever a pre-arranged anecdote is signalled, you ought to preface it with the words:

'I'm so glad you asked me that ...'

or:

'Funny you should ask me that ...'

as this adds to the spontaneity.

There are moments when you should also say to the host:

'Like I said to you before we came on ...'

as this prevents the audience from feeling, in any way, that they are getting served warmed-up left-overs.

As you can imagine, the likelihood of genuine communication in these circumstances is minimal. Hence, you should be very clear in your own mind what you are taking part in the programme for and what it is you want to say.

It frequently happens that people accept invitations to appear on chat shows to plug a book or a film and then completely fail to do so. I was on *Wogan* with Norman Mailer and managed to mention the titles of about seventeen of my books. But poor Norman didn't manage to mention the one he'd flown over on Concorde to plug! His publishers and entourage were nearly suicidal.

So, my advice is to write down on a piece of paper what you want to say, what it is you are plugging – and, if you are ever afflicted by self-doubt, who you are – and put it in your pocket. Should your mind go completely blank, you can always refer to it.

Remember to call the host by his first name. Try very hard to get it right. On the other hand, if you call all chat show hosts:

'Eamonn'

'Michael'

or:

'David'

you are on pretty safe ground. If you get the wrong name, it's good for a laugh. Try pretending to get the wrong name, too. They love it.

Apart from which, you should always begin by saying:

'It's a joy to be here'

or:

'I'm just so pleased to be here.'

If appearing on the BBC you must remember to say:

'And now from my latest album ...'

or:

'This is my latest picture ...'

Name the product and add:

'Oh, I'm not supposed to advertise, am I?'

(It doesn't matter but this is one of the three most deeply ingrained beliefs the public has about the BBC. The others are 1) that you don't mention 'the other side' (commercial TV) because everyone is supposed to be at daggers drawn and 2) that, although the BBC's poverty is well-known, you must expect to be paid handsomely for whatever you do.)

If being interviewed by David Frost – and he makes a joke – you should exclaim:

'Satire!'

If the whole thing is an unmitigated disasters, you are so drunk on hospitality that you fall off the sofa, or whatever, then just reflect philosophically:

'Well, it was nice to be asked!'

(Actually, I'm thinking of using that as the title of my autobiography so, on second thoughts, I'd be grateful if you didn't use it.)

Background notes on this important subject

In the business of book promotion, I have always taken to heart the lesson I learned, metaphorically, at the knee of the late Jacqueline Susann. The woman who gave us such whopping, world-famous best-sellers as *Valley of the Dolls*, and the other one, once said that an author's work did not end when he or she had finished writing a book. That, said the redoubtable self-promoter, was when the author's work *really* began.

And so it was that, after a few years merely nibbling at the promotion of my books within the United Kingdom, I found myself undertaking my first all-out Author Tour – not simply lunching with a journalist now and again, or popping into a radio studio when the mood took me, but twenty-eight days solid of doing nothing else but exposing myself to the media in Australia and New Zealand. (From various hints so far, you may already have guessed that this was where I went.)

Quite why anybody should wish to expose himself to such a tour (or why, having done it, should wish to do it again) is a question I pondered several times during the course of my excursion. But once you are on the roller-coaster there is no getting off. Well, there is, but I don't drink *that* much.

The good thing about promoting anything Down Under is that the Australians make a receptive audience. They are used to being sold to: they even seem to respond to persuasion. There is none of the reserve you encounter in Britain where, if you are not careful, you can be persuaded by the media to take part in a peculiar charade. This consists of your being paid next to nothing, or nothing at all, to provide journalists and broadcasters with 'copy' or programme material on the grounds that they are helping to sell your book. For your part, you have to pretend that you are doing this just for the fun of it and that the last thing you would want them to do is to mention the title of your book. If you are not careful, they won't (see Norman Mailer, above). I will never forget the chill that descended on one BBC studio when an interviewer asked Burt Lancaster, somewhat archly, 'Why are you here in London, Burt?' and Burt replied, 'I'm here to plug my movie.'

My media blitz Down Under began in Sydney with TV appearances on the *Willessee* show (upon which the eponymous host, somewhat curiously, no longer deigned to appear) and the *Mike Walsh Show*. He didn't materialize either. It was hosted by Maggie Taberrer, described as a fashion 'identity' which I took to be an Australianism for 'name' or 'personality'. Then it was time for a round of newspaper and magazine interviews.

The trouble with these is that they take so much longer to do than radio and TV interviews. TV involves make-up and a lot of hanging about in sawdust-lined rooms drinking horrible coffee with researchers – but it can be quite a quick business. Radio, especially 'live' radio, is usually even quicker. Journalists, however, like to take their time. Several rounds of drinks tend to be involved. The journalist likes to tell you *his* life-story and how *he* would have written your book if he had had the time. After a minimum of half an hour, he has taken enough notes to fill several columns. When the article appears, however, he says what he thinks you *ought* to have said, rather than what you actually said, and it takes up six lines.

I began to realize that the real challenge of a promotional tour was not so much physical stamina as the extent to which you could deliver the same old lines as though you had just thought of them.

I was reminded of my own experiences as a broadcaster when I was asking the questions rather than answering them. I was once despatched to interview Kirk Douglas about his latest movie (there seems to be a lot of this going on.) As usual, I had not had enough time to read through the newspaper cuttings before arriving in his suite at the Dorchester, so I flew by the seat of my pants and asked the great star whatever came into my head. He came over as a friendly sort of cove. I can even remember his parting shot. As I pottered off down the hotel corridor, I heard him closing his door. Before he did so, I just heard him turn to his publicity person and say, 'Well, that was a really nice interview …' I imagine he always performs that trick. The more so as, when I did get round to reading through his cuttings, I discovered he had been telling the stories he told me to every interviewer he'd met for the past twenty years. But he is a professional, and, of course, he is an actor, and he can still make them sound morning-fresh.

I flew on to Melbourne. It was there I realized I was not alone in my great enterprise. I had seen the actor George Hamilton being interviewed on TV in Sydney about his latest movie. Here he was in Melbourne answering the same sort of questions – with a good deal of aplomb, let it be said.

Next morning I met yet another of the breed on the hype trail. I had been told to present myself for a half-hour slot on the ABC radio *Front Line* programme … following Stewart Granger, who was plugging a book of his. I became rather anxious when his time in the studio began to encroach on mine. Eventually, however, he was wound up and wheeled out and I was plonked on his warm chair while a record played. By this time it was quite a relief when, admittedly by prior arrangement, I talked much more about the state of British politics than about my books.

The shade of Jacqueline Susann frowned, however. I quote the lady's boast on one occasion: 'No matter what an interviewer brought up, I could work the conversation back to the book.'

Checking into the Oberoi Hotel in Adelaide, who should I see in the lift? Why, George Hamilton, of course, recently arrived to promote his new movie and to answer the same old questions he had answered in Sydney and Melbourne.

Many film actors get lumbered with doing a certain number of days' promotion in return for a hike in their salaries. They then feel they have nothing to gain from the activity. They become moody, bad-tempered and drunk. George looked serene in Adelaide. Mind you, as co-producer, he did have a piece of the action.

As an author, so had I, in a manner of speaking, and if Australia as a whole was open to persuasion, Adelaide positively rolled over and asked to be tickled. A hint of what was to come was to be found on a radio show hosted by Jeremy Cordeaux. When I arrived at the studio, the previous interviewee, a Frenchman, was busy putting away cosmetic samples, having made his sales pitch.

The full force of this rather open use of the media didn't hit me until the next morning when I found myself taking part in a TV programme on the local channel called *A Touch of Elegance.* It was certainly cheap television. Seated in a rather chintzy set was a lady called Margaret Glazbrook. Out of shot was a small audience of old folk, some of whom may possibly have been alive. There was one camera. Then there were the other participants in the programme besides myself. They were all selling something and they had all brought their samples with them.

The form was for the camera to go into a close-up of Margaret while each of us slipped in turn into the vacant seat next to her. Then the camera pulled back to show us and our wares (mine were my books, of course.) Before me there had been a woman promoting Givenchy. After me was a person flogging handbags. Just possibly this was what John Logie Baird had in mind when he was inventing television.

On the morning I checked out of my hotel in Adelaide I happened to notice a piece of paper flapping over the switchboard. It said that on no account were telephone calls to be put through to Mr Stewart Granger's room until further notice, except from his publisher. Oh dear, I did hope the poor fellow wasn't about to fall by the wayside …

To Brisbane: no sign of Stewart Granger or George Hamilton. But as I was being ushered out of one set-up, coming in were Buck's Fizz, the singing group who had made a name for themselves in Britain but, at that time, were virtually unknown in Australia. By the reception desk at another TV station, I overheard a girl explaining to the receptionist that she had come to plug the Women's Harlots Association. The accent misled me, I'm afraid. I later found out she was from the Women's Pilot's Association. The studio had already been visited by Buck's Fizz and, the day before, Topol had been through promoting a movie, his autobiography and anything else he could think of.

By now my interview count was up to thirty-nine and it was time to move on to New Zealand. The chat show scene is more restrained there. Whereas in Australia I found myself welcomed by people saying, 'Jeez, Nige, pleased to meet ya! What a great book, fantastic!' or interviewed by people who would pick up my books and wave them at the TV camera saying, 'Go out and buy these books, you won't regret it, they're great!' I soon discovered that New Zealanders did not want to be sold to directly. They would buy your book in great quantities (they are great readers) but they did not want to be persuaded. The media reaction tended to be, 'Oh, well, thank you for coming.'

I also signed some copies at a bookshop – something Jacqueline Susann would not have deigned to do, quite rightly. She gave up signing sessions when an ugly character came up and whispered in her ear, 'Wanna fuck, Jackie?'

So to Wellington and my final and fifty-second interview. I think I had just about got it right by then. I knew how to deal with criticism (agree with it) and how to tease. But I had to ask myself – what was the value of all this frenetic activity by George and Stewart and Topol and Buck's Fizz and me? Lord Leverhulme, the soap king, once said that fifty per cent of his advertising was wasted but no one knew which fifty per cent. The same, I suppose, goes for promotion – though the effectiveness may well be less than fifty per cent. There are moments, though, when you know your peculiar progress is having results. A publisher's rep was going about his business in Hobart, Tasmania, when a woman burst in and said, 'I've just seen this man called

Nigel Rees on the *Mike Walsh Show*. Have you got any of his books?' At such moments the shade of Jacqueline Susann must smile.

So, it's on with the TV suit, pause at the top of the stairs, and 'Will you welcome ...' once again. Don't forget what I've told you to say. You know it makes sense.

Having Sex

There is a school of thought which has it that sex should be performed in deep silence, certainly without any attendant whoops or titters. Recent research has shown, on the contrary, that satisfaction is heightened by the amount of polite conversation that goes on during the event. I can personally vouch for the enhancement of the sexual act after a loved one has casually dropped in such nuggets as:

'Have you seen where the new Sainsbury's is going to be?'

or:

'George, the ceiling needs painting!'

So here are some suggestions for fervour-increasing comments that you may care to make before, during or after the event. As this is such a large subject, other, more specialist tastes, will be found catered for in REFLECTING ON ASPECTS OF SEXUALITY.

Before:

HE: **'What's your action?'** ('How do you want it?')

HE: **'LS/MFT'** ('Let's screw, my finger's tired.')

(American readers may be surprised by this explanation for those well-known initials found on cigarette packets.)

About to:

HE: **'The things I do for England ...'**

During:

HE: **'You are an A1 tumble-bun!'**

(This comes recommended by John D. Eichenlaub MD in his seminal work *The Marriage Art* and is laboratory-designed, so he says, to 'increase feminine fervour'. We can be sure it does.)

HE: **'Relax ...'**

After:

HE: **'Was it good/OK/beautiful for you, too?'**

HE: **'You've made an old man very happy!'**

HE: **'On a scale of one to ten, how was I?'**

HE: **'I wouldn't have you any other way.'**

HE: **'Wham, bam, thank you, ma'am!'**

SHE: **'Thank you for having me.'**

Now wash your hands.

Introducing People

I am a great believer, when introducing people, in providing a little bit of biographical information, or at least some pointer, to enable the newly-introduced to buckle down to some hard conversation straight away.

Try:

'This is ——. He thinks the sun shines out of your arse-hole'

or:

'Look who's crawled out of the woodwork'

or:

'Look what the tide's brought in ...'

This enables one of the parties to the introduction to say:

'—— has told me so much about you ...'

– which is very reassuring.

I would recommend for your guidance the way I was once introduced to the famous and talented medical person, Dr Miriam Stoppard. This was in the days before she married her present husband and was known by another name. Nevertheless, she still had a formidable reputation in the pharmaceutical world.

'This,' said the person who introduced us, 'is Dr Miriam Moore-Robinson:

'She has the largest collection of condoms this side of the Iron Curtain.'

The conversation got off to a wonderful start and we have been chums ever since.

I have often wondered, though, and never seem to get round to asking Miriam: who has the largest collection of condoms on the other side of the Iron Curtain?

Laying It On With A Trowel

It is not just enough for people to call each other the cat's pyjamas, the bee's knees or the kipper's knickers. To women, men should say:

'You are more like an angel than a woman'

or:

'I should like my roses to see you.'

To employers, grovelling workers should say:

'If you grant me a pay rise, I will forever pray to the Lord Jesus Christ whom you so greatly resemble.'

To senior officers:

'Drake, Nelson and … I didn't quite catch your name, sir?'

To newly-delivered mothers:

'Now that's what I call a baby!'

In response to all these effusions, recipients should say:

'Flattery will get you everywhere!'

Lying On Your Deathbed

With the family gathered round you, straining to pick up your last words, you should say either:

''Ere, who's looking after the whelk-stall?'

or:

'Boo!'

Making Charitable Appeals

When making an appeal, say on radio's *The Week's Good Cause*, you should talk about 'caring and sharing' and make frequent references to 'this worthy cause'.

You should end with:

'Please send all you can, however small, to me at this address ... Thank you, and goodnight.'

Gentlemen of the road should, however, adopt the technique once used on me when I was an undergraduate at Oxford. A tramp of Irish descent approached and made as if to shake me by the hand. He began:

'May I have the honour, sir, to shake the hand of a gentleman and a scholar of the University of Oxford?'

When he had done so, he added:

'And could you spare me sixpence for a cup of tea?'

Use this form, or 'a scholar and a gentleman' or 'an officer and a gentleman', according to circumstances. See if it does you any more good than it did him.

Making Excuses

I have come across many vivid excuses in my time. The best excuse I have heard for a person being late for a radio interview (apart from the obvious ones like 'my wife was having a baby' and 'I was attending my grandmother's funeral') was from Phillip Knightley, the journalist. He said:

'I've just been to my son's circumcision.'

This can be safely recommended for use by almost anybody.

Also in radio, I remember Ronald Fletcher fluffing his lines something terrible on one occasion, before breaking off to explain to the audience:

'You must forgive me ... my wife has flu.'

When I fluff my lines, I tend to resort to the useful:

'Sorry, my pace-maker needs a new battery.'

(People are always very sympathetic.)

The best excuse for declining to join a woman who has 'got religion' and asks 'Shall we pray?' is probably:

'No, I've just Hoovered the carpet.'

When declining to do absolutely anything, say:

'No, I can't. I've got a bone in my leg.'

This enables people to comment, warmly, that:

'You're sitting there with your teeth all in your mouth and your elbow half-way up your arm.'

Pay no attention to them.

Negotiating

The standard mode of negotiation, given the excellent state of management/union relations in the country, is for the union to demand something like:

'We want an across-the-board improvement, cash on the table, upfront – and then we put our snouts in the trough.'

But, with a little care, some slightly more effective and fruitful negotiating ploys may be brought into use on both sides.

Begin by saying:

'Let's talk turkey'

or:

'Let's get down to brass tacks.'

One side must then make an offer in order to start the negotiating process. Whoever makes it must accompany it with the words:

'And that is absolutely our final offer ... there is nothing left in the kitty, believe me.'

The other side should then counter with any of the following lines, often all at once:

'You must be joking!'
'Don't let's play silly buggers ...'
'We're not working for a bloody charity, you know ...'
'Frankly, it'd be cheap at half the price ...'
'We are prepared to hold out to the nth degree ...'

I had an agent long ago who would express total horror at whatever measly pittance the BBC was offering me for my services and declare:

'Well, I'm afraid the BBC's going to have to dig a little deeper into its purse, dear!'

Or perhaps it was 'piggy-bank'? Either will do. This was most effective and usually resulted in the offer of another half-guinea (yes, we're talking about that long ago).

At a similar point (i.e. improvement) in any negotiation, say warmly:

'Now you're talking …'

but add, quickly:

'Nevertheless, there are one or two points I don't think have been covered …'

Say soothingly:

'I don't think this is going to cost you an arm and a leg …'

Never resort to:

'Fuck you, Jack, I'm all right …'

Give in eventually and sign off, generously, by reflecting:

'I don't know what things are coming to. We had to settle for half-a-crown and a packet of tea'

and:

'Ah, well, anything for a quiet life!'

Represent this as a total triumph to yourself or to anyone you are representing.

Nudge-Nudging

Some of you, I know, will be rather shocked by the directness of approach displayed in such sections of this book as CHATTING UP, HAVING SEX, DINING AT BUCKINGHAM PALACE, and so on. Hence, this quiet oasis in which I will expound the gentler charms of nudge-nudging. By this, I mean the art of conversation when both parties know what they are on about but aren't too terribly explicit about it.

It is possible for entire, three-hour-long conversations to be conducted in nudge-nudge, but here is just a short sample of the sort of exchanges I have in mind.

The parties should greet each other with:

'We must stop meeting like this!'

The main body of the conversation should consist of them saying:

'If you know what I mean – and I'm pretty sure you do!'

The parties should take some time in saying farewell:

'Take care – and don't do anything I wouldn't do!'

is absolutely mandatory – as is:

'Be good – and if you can't be good, be careful – and if you can't be careful, buy a pram!'

– though the last part may be pushing it a bit.

Observing Male Ballet Dancers

On first catching sight of a male ballet dancer, it is absolutely mandatory for male members of the audience to exclaim:

'Ah, I see he's brought his sandwiches with him!'

Playing Games

I may not be the best person to offer advice in this area. After all, it once said on my school report: 'RUGBY – Nigel's chief contribution is his presence on the field'. But I have had the last laugh. Now that my games-excelling contemporaries, heads of cricket, football and all that, are being wheeled about in bath-chairs, I am the possessor of the gorgeous body that you see before you now.

I may have been a champion of the Great Indoors when it comes to sport but at least I do know what to say on the touch-line or when watching it on TV:

'Good shot!'
'Good stroke!'
'Come on, Jesus, get stuck in!'
'Play up, play up, and play the game!'
'May the best man win!'
'It's not whether you won or lost, but how you played the game ...'
'Keep a straight bat.'
'Take it on the chin.'
'Don't pull your punches.'
'You're the pits of the world!'
'It's a funny game, football.'

– the list goes on for ever.

In addition, I am able to give a first-hand account of what to say when playing croquet with the wife of the Warden of an Oxford college, which may be of some interest to you. Towards the end of my time at Oxford I was invited to tea with the Warden, the Warden's wife and the Warden's somewhat Marxist-inclined daughter. As I recall, we had it out on the lawn, I managed to pour tea all over my No 1 trousers, and the Warden's wife, who was famous for non-stop chatter, chattered non-stop.

(She had once been observed coming out of chapel, talking non-stop, with nobody beside her. On another occasion she had asked an assembly of freshman who had gone to see some of the college's treasures, 'Now, has everybody seen my chest?' But I digress.)

The Warden's wife had obviously done a bit of homework and asked at one point, 'Now, Rees, you're involved in show business, aren't you ... you play the *guitar*!' (Well, near enough, I suppose ...)

It was to try to prevent any more of this that I gladly acquiesced to a game of croquet on the Warden's somewhat bumpy lawn. I was none too sure of the rules but that did not seem to matter as the Warden's wife was very encouraging. If I took a dreadful swipe at the ball and it ended up in the flower-bed, she would say:

'Oh, *forceful* shot!'

If, on the other hand, I swung the mallet and tapped the ball with such lack of force that it barely moved, she would exclaim:

'Oh, *subtle* shot!'

I pass these on in case they should be of any use to you.

Before I stop, I might add that there has been a new development in sport as far as the players themselves are concerned. There was a time when players played and commentators did all the talking. Not so nowadays. A new generation of players is coming up whose first experience of sport has been through watching it on TV. As a result, they expect there to be a commentary, even if there isn't one. And if there isn't, they must supply one for themselves.

I first became aware of this trend when I observed my

young nephew kicking a ball around the garden on his own and saying things to himself like, 'Superb shot! ... Is he going to do it? ... Yes, he is! ... Absolutely superb!'

I shall have to warn him against saying things like:

'He's pulling out the big one now'

and:

'He opens wide his legs and shows his class'

as these should only be employed by readers of this book.

Presenting The Prizes

The form is usually the same: a letter arrives at your home, that of a distinguished person, and it starts: 'Although you do not know me personally ...' It is from the headmaster of a school who is planning his Open Day/Speech Day/Prize-Giving several months hence, 'at which some well-known celebrity usually comes to present the prizes and to be our guest ... To give you some idea of the sort of people who have honoured us by their presence, I list some of the most recent ones: Lord Tedder, the late Rt. Hon. Sir Stafford Cripps, Air Chief Marshal Sir Augustus Walker, Air Vice Marshal Colin Lamb, the Rt. Hon. Kenneth Robinson, Nicholas Winterton MP, and Sir Robin Day of the BBC ... If by any chance you can come on that date, I should be delighted ...'

Note that there is no mention of your making a speech – nor of half-holidays. But a few well-chosen words are indeed expected of you and, of course, you accept.

Then the nightmare begins. What on earth are you going to say? Have no fears! *The Gift Of The Gab* will see you through. In rather more detail than other sections, here is what you should say ...

Remember, you have just been presenting the prizes, so a couple of witty ad libs about that will do to begin with:

'Mr Chairman, Ladies and Gentlemen, boys of the school ... I have never been called "Sir" so many times in my life before! They say you know you are getting older when policemen start looking younger. Well, I have another yardstick: you know you're getting older when Popes start looking younger than you are!

'Thank you, Mr Chairman, for your kind introduction. **Having heard all the nice things you said about me, I can't wait to hear myself speak!** I know I must engage the attention of all of you this afternoon. If I fail, I will know immediately. I will see your eyes wandering towards the windows, as mine did when I was at school so long ago. I will hear the shuffle of your feet and your coughs. And I will know only too well when some awful first-former starts to carve his initials on the back of the boy in front of him.

'My dilemma is this: **I never won any prizes when I was at school. I was always bottom of the form**. So, what can I say today which will be of any use to any of you? What can I say to the parents, who are all trying so hard to appear intelligent and well-behaved? What can I say to the staff, who have heard it all before, anyway? And what I can say to you, the boys, who have only a very dim idea of who I am?

'There is always the terrible temptation on occasions like this to appeal to the lowest common denominator; but, today, I am going to address myself to the highest common factor – which is you, the boys. For without you, this school would not exist; without you, the staff would have to find proper jobs; and, without you, your parents would be considerably better off.

'But, having taken the decision "Who to address?", I am now faced with an even greater problem, "What am I to say?"

'If I were the kind of distinguished old buffer who usually gets invited to present the prizes, I would no doubt say something to the effect: "Heavens, I wish I were in your shoes! **I would not presume to teach my grandmother to suck eggs**, but may I point out that your whole life is spread out before you! How I remember my own schooldays!" – wait for it, here it comes – "They were the happiest days of my life …"

'But I can't say that, because being an honest sort of

chap, I have to tell you that I don't envy you in the least! **I don't claim to know everything – my modesty is proverbial** – but I went to a perfectly good school and I couldn't wait to finish my formal education and start earning a living – **because that's when the learning really starts.**

'However, I don't suppose that's a very helpful thing to tell you in your present position, because you're unlikely to be out of all this before 1992, even with remission for good behaviour. So I won't say it.

'And, you know, there is something terribly wrong if your schooldays *are* the happiest days of your life. They should be no more than a preparation for it. If you go to a good school – and I'm assuming for the sake of argument that you do – it should whet your appetite for the good things that life has to offer. School should introduce you to more than text-book knowledge. However painful the experience, it should teach you about people. **Far be it from me to suggest**, but you might even learn something from the staff! And one day in the distant future when you meet up with them again, and you have grown up and they haven't, you'll find them really quite human.

'So, as you can see, I'm not really the sort of person who usually stands up and holds forth on speech days. But I do share one thing with the distinguished old buffers I dimly remember dishing out the prizes when I was at school: it makes you think back. It makes *me* think back and wonder what *I* would like to have heard when, **instead of standing up here, I was sitting down there, where you are now …**

'Well, I'll tell you. I wanted someone to come along on speech day and tell me that, yes, I could one day end up doing the job I wanted to do. I wanted someone to come along on speech day and tell me that games didn't matter! I hated games so much that on Wednesdays and on Saturdays I used to *pray* that it would rain. And, you know, sometimes it worked … and we had to play games in the rain!

'That's what I would like to have heard. But I don't suppose I'd better say it to you today either.

'Now, to be serious just for a moment, I suppose I ought to pause and wonder what the chairman and the headmaster and your parents would like me to say.

[*Insert view for or against state/private education*]

'I've said that for the parents and staff. Not many laughs, but there you are. And I've told you what *I* would like to have heard from a speech day speech.

'Finally, I am faced with the question – what would *you* like me to say? It occurs to me that what you would most like to hear from me about – and this is probably the sole reason for my visit – is on the subject of half-holidays.

'Well, the good news is that you are going to get one. And the bad news is that it's to be on 25 December! No, I'm sure it can be fitted in some time when you will really notice it. And now that I am the most popular man in the hall, I will sit down.'

It is quite simple really. Feel free to use it if ever you get the call.

Protecting The Innocent

In the Preface, I mentioned something called 'Aunt Addie's "Poison" Remark' as an example of verbal combustion technique – i.e. one capable of getting a conversation going in the most difficult of circumstances. This is true, but I feel bound to point out that the poison remark was intended, at bottom, to have quite a different function, namely, to inform the adults present whilst protecting the innocent young.

Another correction: she was really a Great Aunt. Most of her life was spent residing in suites at hotels in the country. She was a widow of some wealth – most of which she seemed to spend on white face powder. This was particularly noticeable when she kissed you and vast deposits of the stuff crashed down on to her silk dress with all the force and terror of avalanches on the Matterhorn.

Be that as it may, in my short-trousered days, Great Aunt Addie came on a visit and wished to impart to my parents how some mutual acquaintance had passed away. Except that 'passed away' was not quite revealing enough. Looking at my brother and me, and wishing to protect our dear, sweet, innocent, little minds, Great Aunt Addie dropped her face suddenly, causing another tumultuous avalanche of face powder, and made to say under her breath, the forbidden word:

'POISON!'

Alas, we heard it all too clearly, thanks to the excellence of her theatrical whisper, and my life has been blighted ever since.

I forget now what the moral of this anecdote was supposed to be, but you are probably old enough to work it out for yourself.

Putting People Down

This book is designed to appeal to all tastes and to cover all eventualities. And so, distasteful though it may be to some, we must now move on to the question of what to say when you want your conversational partner to understand that you do not hold him in the highest regard.

I can only present you with these barbs in the hope that you will not find it necessary to use them. If you do, then please exercise all delicacy in their deployment …

Bores:

'How interesting! Why don't you go away and write it all down?!'

'A period of silence on your part would be appreciated …'

Personal Remarks:

'There is such a thing as manners, you know …'

'Go and take a running jump at yourself …'

'Don't just do something, stand there!'

'If you dropped five bob down the lavatory, you'd pull out a gold watch …'

'Well, you're not backward in coming forward ...'

'Pull the other one, it's got bells on ...'

'Who's got a bag of chips on his shoulder, then?'

'Amuse yourself – don't mind me ...'

'I wouldn't trust you as far as I could throw you ...'

'Get back on your jam-jar ...'

Criticizing Clothes:

'Such lovely stockings – I can't wait for them to come back into fashion!'

'Tell me the history of that dress ...'

'Oh, are you *really* wearing that?'

Meanies:

'He throws money about like a man with no arms.'

Watery Speakers:

'Say it, don't spray it ...'

Wet Third Parties:

'He doesn't know his arse from his elbow.'

'He's like a wet dream in technicolour.'

'He's as soft/daft as a brush.'

'They're so confused, they're stabbing each other in the chest.'

Persons Claiming Still To Be Virgins:

'Virgin on the ridiculous, if you ask me ...'

Denis Healey, a charming Labour politician, recommends that you preface all these expressions with his favourite phrase:

'With respect ...'

If any of these fail, simply remark:

'The answer's in the plural – and they bounce.'

Recovering with Aplomb

If you have put your foot in it, the only thing to do is brazen it out. Remember, particularly, my advice on dealing with hecklers: agree with them. This is the key. So, for example, if you have just been slagging off some well-known local figure and the pretty but blushing girl in the corner volunteers that she is his daughter then all you can say is,

'Then you'll know exactly what I mean!'

I have also been given an excellent example of recovery with aplomb which is well worth treasuring up:

MAN A: 'All the students at —— University are either football players or whores.'

MAN B: My wife is a student there!'

MAN A: 'Oh, really? **What position does she play?'**

Superb!

Reflecting On Aspects of Sexuality

A lot of people don't do it, they just talk about it.

'I wouldn't mind giving her one'

'I wouldn't mind getting inside his trousers'

is usually about as far as it goes. So here are some lively and original things for you to say in this field:

On frequency and timing:

'Once a knight, always a knight: twice a night and you're doing all right ...'

'The best fucks are always after a good cry.'

On men as sexual objects:

'He's got a liberal allowance ...'

'Look at that wedding tackle ...'

'He's what you'd call small but perfectly formed.'

'Knowing him, he'll be at it till sparrows fart.'

'Small feet, small cock.'

'Big conk, big cock.'

'He's no Adonis.'

'He's always going for the groceries.'

'He was in like Flynn.'

On women as sexual objects:

'I believe in the three Fs – feed 'em, fuck 'em, forget 'em.'

'I believe in the four Fs – find, feel, fuck and forget.'

'They all look the same in the dark.'

'She makes love with her gloves on, you know – so messy!'

'She should lie back and enjoy it ...'

'Big conk, big cunt.'

'Kissing her is like kissing a brick wall.'
'She's got nipples bigger than my wife's tits.'
'She wouldn't know if you'd been up her with an armful of armchairs.'
'I bet she's a real go-er.'
'She has a Rolls Royce body and a Balham mind' (thank you, Beachcomber).

On being interrupted on the job:
'Ah, vicar, there you are!'
'I haven't a thing to wear!'
'Nice day we're having!'
'Good evening vicar!'
'Sorry, dear – got tied up at the office!'
'I don't think you've met my wife …!'

On interrupting others in flagrante:
'Can anyone join in?'
'This is where we came in, dear.'
'I thought you were in – and I can see you are!'
'Is there room in there for a small one?'

On preferences:
'I'm a tit man myself.'
'Love me, love my dog.'
'If you can't join 'em, beat 'em.'
'It's the most fun you can have with your clothes on.' (Leather and rubber-wear fanciers only.)

On coitus interruptus:
'We'll have to get off at Edge Hill' (Liverpool)
'We'll have to get off at Haymarket' (Edinburgh)
'We'll have to get off at Redfern' (Sydney).

On the curse:
'My little friend has come.'
'Auntie's been.'
'I have friends to stay.'
'Kit has come.'
'I have the rags on.'
'I have the painters in.'
'The captain is at home.'
' "The curse is come upon me", cried The Lady of Shalott.'

On fat lovers:
'Just slap her and ride in on the waves.'

'She's got a bottom like two ferrets fighting in a sack.'

On readiness:

'He'd shag anything on two legs.'
'She'd ride a bike if it had a knob on.'
'He'd fuck a hedgehog if it didn't have spikes on.'
'She's had more pricks than a pin cushion.'
'She bangs like a shit-house door in a gale.'
'She's the town bike – ridden by everybody.'
'She's had more rides than Lester Piggott.'

On rejecting marriage:

'Why buy a book when you can join a library?'
'Why keep a cow when you can buy milk/climb over the fence?'

On older women:

'She's not so young as she was ...'
'They don't yell, they don't tell, and they're very, very grateful.'

On what to say to flashers:

'I've seen better ...'
'It looks like a cock, only smaller ...'

On it all, when it's over:

'Did you bed her then?'
'Hole in one, dear boy!'
'It was like shaking hands with a pair of rubber gloves on.'
'It was like trying to open an oyster with a bus ticket.'
'All the world and his ex-wife were there.'

On sexuality in general:

'It's not what it's cracked up to be.'

And the World Said:

'You *didn't*, you dirty dog!'

Rejecting Amorous Advances

When wishing to show a man or woman who is chatting you up that 1) you have no time for him/her, 2) that you are not interested in having a date, or 3) that you have no wish to go to bed with him/her, use any combination of these:

1) **'I bet you say that to all the girls/boys …'**
   'I'm not like other guys' (courtesy of Michael Jackson)
   'You've got a one-track mind.'
2) **'I must introduce you to my mother …'**
   'Would you mind if I brought my friend along'*
   'I've got to stay in and wash my hair …'
3) **'I want a bloke not a joke …'**
   'Sorry, mate, I think you'd need jump leads …'
   'I'd love to, really, but I wouldn't want to harm the baby …'
   'Not tonight, Josephine.'
   ''Ere, did you have garlic for lunch?'
   'No, you can't. Once you've seen one, you've seen both.'

The most devastating way of dealing with annoying would-be seducers who say, 'I'd like to make love to you' is to reply, firmly:

'Well, if you do, and I ever get to hear about it, I shall be very cross indeed.'

Responding To *Double Entendres*

If you suspect that an act of *double entendre* has been committed, either by yourself or another, there are a number of appropriate comments that you can make. For example, traditionally, a bishop says to a schoolgirl who is about to take part in an all-female production of *A Midsummer Night's Dream*: 'I'm so looking forward to it, this is the first time I've seen a female Bottom.' At this point, either you, or the bishop, if he is very ecumenical, should add:

'As the bishop said to the actress …' (being the most common expression, or:)

'As the art mistress said to the gardener …' (try this occasionally for variety.)

* Do not specify the nature of the friend at this stage – whether dumpy flat-mate, seven foot life-guard, or miniature horse.

To make things a little clearer, let me supply some *double entendres* and appropriate responses:

To apply to your own double entendres:

'I wonder if you could get me going **... if you take my meaning ...'**

'I have often wondered whether yours is bigger than mine **... I'm sorry, I'll read that again ...'**

'Shall we go upstairs and put our things together **... er, if I may re-phrase that ...'**

'The vicar asked me to press his pants **... so to speak ... in the nicest possible sense, of course!'**

'This is where his Lordship holds his balls and dances **... or words to that effect ...'**

'I have often had the pleasure **...in more senses than one ...'**

'Mrs Stokes and I have been sharing the same address for some time **... and not a word to the vicar!'**

To apply to the double entendres *of others*:

'I'm going to give her one and take down her particulars ...'
'But not necessarily in that order ...'

'He said he was always very pleased when the vicar came ...'
'In the words of the prophet!'

'Excuse me, but have you ever had a nasty lump ...?'
'Ask a silly question ...!'

'She said she was always keen to give you a helping hand ...'
'I should be so lucky ...!'

'Come to bed, darling, I've got to be up first thing ...'
'Promises, promises!'

Saying Hail And Farewell

In addition to those examples given under OPENING GAMBITS and UNWANTED GUESTS, here are some other intriguing ways of saying Hail or Farewell, always provided, of course, that you know whether you are coming or going:

HAIL

'Haven't seen you for ages!'
'Long time no see!'
'Top o' the mornin'!'
'Hands off cocks, on with socks!'
'Look what the cat's brought in!'
'What's new, pussycat?'
'Is everybody happy!'
'Hello, good evening and welcome!'

FAREWELL

'Have a nice day!'
'It may never happen!'
'T.T.F.N.!'
'All good things must come to an end!'
'Duty calls!'
'Must be getting along now!'
'I must love you and leave you!'
'I must go on my way rejoicing!'
'Time and tide wait for no man!'
'Another day, another dollar!'
'Be seeing you!'
'Look after yourself!'
'Back to the grindstone!'
'Take care!'
'Love to the wife and the kids!'
'Love to your very lovely lady wife!'
'My name is Walker!'
'Keep smiling!'
'See you soon!'

'Bye for now!'
'I think I'll call it a day!'
'Must be off!'
'See you later, alligator!'
'I'll see you anon!'
'So long then!'
'I'll be toddling along then!'
'It's been nice meeting you!'
'Good hunting!'

(*Exeunt omnes.*)

I thought they'd never go.

Someone Breaks Wind

With the advent of the F-Plan Diet and similar shirt-lifting experiences, it is important to be able to cope with the incidence of farting, which threatens to be of epidemic proportions these days.

Should you be the culprit, *on no account should you own up or apologize.* The reason for this is best illustrated by the story told concerning President Gowon, the Nigerian leader, who came to Britain on a State Visit. Welcomed by the Queen at Victoria Station, he had barely sat down in a carriage for the short drive to Buckingham Palace, when one of the horses let rip with an ear-splitting tail-lifter. The Queen was very put out by this, as well she might be, and turned to President Gowon, saying, 'Oh, I do apologize … not a very good start to your visit!' Replied he: 'Oh, please don't apologize … besides, I thought it was one of the horses …'

No, never apologize. Someone is bound to make a literary allusion along the lines of:

'Wastes his sweetness on the desert air …'

or exclaim:

'Foggy on the river tonight!'

– and this will be quite adequate. This last may also be said in response to tummy rumblings, especially among the elderly.

Should burping be the problem, you can train yourself to say:

'Archbishops!'

to cover the explosion, though this does, of course, require considerable presence of mind. An intriguing and colourful variation on this method is to recite a list of Surrey towns, viz.:

'Oxshott,
'Aldershot,
'Stoke d'Abernon …'

whenever an outburst is about to occur.

Swearing

Should you ever find yourself letting out a swear word in inappropriate surroundings (cf. DINING AT BUCKINGHAM PALACE) there are one or two ways in which you can minimize the offence, viz. by the addition of a stock phrase. For example:

'Hell! – **as the Duchess said when she caught her tit in the mangle …!'**
'I mean, shit! – **Scout's Honour!'**
'Fucking Ada – **if you'll pardon my French …!'**
'*Merde*! – **and cross my heart and hope to die!'**

Be careful when inventing your own swear words. Princess Anne would have been well advised to find out what the word 'naff' meant before saying to photographers:

'Why don't you naff off!'

Talking Loudly At The Theatre

This takes considerable skill as there is always someone sitting behind you ready to dig you in the back with a deafening 'Sssssssshhhhh!' Simply get your line out in as loud a voice as you can, and continue unwrapping your boiled sweets very methodically, or waiting for your digital watch to sound the next hour.

Comments should be as closely related as possible to what is happening on stage, e.g. during *Macbeth*:

'That reminds me, the blood donor people are coming on Thursday.'

This sort of thing instantly sets up a kind of bond between audience and actor.

My mother once overheard two old biddies as they watched me stutter my way through the part of Marlow in Goldsmith's *She Stoops to Conquer*. After I had been doing this for some time, one turned to the other and said:

'Oh, poor boy, they shouldn't let him act ...'

I laughed haversacks at this.

Only occasionally is it permissible to speak to the performers on stage. For example, if the hero has to pick up his beloved in his arms, and is clearly having a bit of difficulty doing so, it is quite in order to call out:

'Take what you can, luv, and come back for the rest!'

If the heroine has just died and the hero is wondering aloud what he is going to do without her, it is a pleasant touch to advise him audibly:

'Shag her while she's still warm!'

This may endear you to the rest of the audience, if not to the actors. It also works very well at the opera.

Throwing Up In Australia

Australia might seem rather a long way to go in order to be sick but there is a special reason for this, which I will come to in a moment. First, let me say that:

'I'm going to be sick!'

is one of the most vital expressions contained in this entire book. It is extremely useful, say, when you are stuck in a crowded place and want to get out quickly. It works like a charm. The crowd simply melts away, rather like the Red Sea dividing.

In Australia, however, they have exercised considerable imagination in devising colourful ways of describing this great human event. If you have read thus far in the book we must assume that you are a lover of language and are prepared to go to any lengths in order to exercise the gift of the gab. And there is hardly any length longer than going to Australia.

The equivalent expressions Down Under for 'I'm going to be sick' include:

'I'm going to …

do a technicolour yawn
cry ruth (the last word pronounced raspingly)
talk on the big white telephone (imagine it!)
enjoy myself in reverse
pebbledash a bungalow
park a tiger (cf. the Sloane Ranger 'park a custard')
yodel on the lawn
do a liquid laugh
chunder.'

After it is all over and you have returned from doing it Down Under, Sloane Rangers will remark:

'He lost his fodder in the thunderbowl.'

What more lasting tribute to human achievement could there be?

Viewing TV

It is very important to keep up a stream of interesting comments when watching TV with other people. Concerning male newscasters, a suitable remark would be:

'That's a nice tie he's wearing.'

When people have the same surname you should wonder aloud:

'I wonder if Ginger Rogers **is related to** Roy Rogers?'

When actors come on the screen, at particularly gripping moments in the drama, exclaim loudly:

'Doesn't he take his part well?'

or ask your companions:

'Wasn't he married to that girl who used to appear in *Crossroads*?'

(In all likelihood he will have been.)

Visiting Stately Homes

There is really only one thing you can say if you are visiting a stately home as a member of the ticket-buying general public, viz.:

'I bet this takes a lot of dusting!'

I have heard this delivered with great effect at Chatsworth, Knole, Hatfield, and Beaulieu. You should say it, too.

More adventurous souls should say of the present owner, in a loud voice:

'He was born with a silver foot in his mouth!'

– which should go down equally well.

Should you happen to have the privilege of actually meeting His Grace, it is mandatory for you to say:

'Nice little place you've got here, your Lordship!'

(See also DINING AT BUCKINGHAM PALACE. For heaven's sake, how did you miss it? You're not skipping, are you?)

Wanting To Annoy Someone

I have a clear memory of walking through a public park in Penarth, Glamorgan, in the 1950s and hearing someone behind me shout:

'Hey!'

On turning round, I received the rest of the message:

'... Mambo!'

This was the title of a popular song of the period, I should point out. The perpetrator of this jest was, I am almost sure, what would have been called at the time a 'Teddy Boy'.

Subsequently, I learned a variation. You would go up behind people, usually of the opposite sex, not too close, of course, and hail them with:

'Hey there!'

When they turned round, you would croon:

'... you with the stars in your eyes!'

This was also the title of a popular song of the period. Is it not time that these venerable war-horses were brought back?

The traditional form of this kind of annoyance gambit is to call out to cyclists:

'Hey mate ... your back wheel's going round!'

The more modern variant is to honk your horn at Volvo drivers and call out:

'Excuse me, your lights are on!'

Wanting To Be Colourful

Care should be taken not to over-egg your talk with the following metaphors and similes. But, sparingly used, they will brighten it up no end.

I can recall very clearly the occasion when I first heard the expression:

'With your thumb in your bum and your mind in neutral'

– it was said by a Sandhurst-trained army officer to describe an aspect of military alertedness in 1961. We were stationed at the time in Magilligan camp, Co. Londonderry, Northern Ireland. 'I must use that sometime,' I said to myself. The very next day I could see that there were indeed worse things than having your thumb in your bum etc.

I spent a night in a tent with some army cadet colleagues up in the hills. Whether through negligence, incompetence or sheer necessity, we had had to pitch our tent on a slope in the middle of a stream, so that water trickled down our sleeping bags with the utmost discomfort. I wish that I had known then the invaluable expression:

'Bitched, buggered and bewildered (like Barney's bull)'

– which would have summed up our position very well. Anyway.

Take note of these:

Reassuring 'better than' comparisons:

'Well, it's better than a slap round the face with a wet kipper.'

'Well, it's better than a slap in the belly with a wet fish.'

'Well, it's better than a poke in the eye with a sharp stick.'

'Well, it's better than a night in bed with a dead policeman.'

Interesting nervous comparisons:

'He's as nervous as a long-tailed cat in a roomful of rocking chairs ...'

'He's as nervous as a cat on a hot tin roof.'

'He's as jumpy as a one-legged cat in a sandbox.'

Intimations of loneliness:

'He's as lonesome as a peanut in a box.'

'He was standing about like a spare prick at a wedding.'

'He was standing about like a ham sandwich at a Jewish wedding.'

'He fitted in like a pork chop at a synagogue.'

Indications of difficulty:

'It's about as easy as juggling with soot.'

Suggestions of inadequacy:

'He wouldn't know how to run a whelk stall.'

'He couldn't organize a piss-up in a brewery.'

'He couldn't organize a fuck/an orgy in a brothel.'

'He couldn't sell ice water in hell.'

'He couldn't punch his way out of a paperbag.'

'He couldn't knock the skin off a rice pudding.'

Tasteful comparisons:

'It's as common as cat-shit and twice as nasty.'

'I'm as busy as a one-armed paper-hanger.'

'He's as bald as a badger's bum.'

'You're as useless as tits on a canary.'

'Oh, I wouldn't do that. It's a bit like wanking in your soup, isn't it?'

(I think we'd better stop there, don't you?'

Wanting To Be Offensive

It is but a short step from the foregoing to what we are standing in at the moment. Should you feel the need to refrain from mincing words, and in no way should the existence of this section be taken as an endorsement of such a posture, you might care to make use of the following very offensive expressions:

'Get out and milk yourself' (best said to motorists who are unlikely to follow your advice).

'Stop buzzing round like a blue-arsed fly.'

'You must be out of your tiny Chinese mind.' (Expect complaints from the highly-respected and extremely clever Chinese community, if you stoop to this one.)

Say to butch males:

'You prawn!' (a prawn has no private parts, you see)

and:

'Don't come the raw prawn with me …'

or:

'… with knobs on!'

and:

''Ere, are you looking for a punch up the bracket?'

or:

'I'll have your guts for garters.'

(The author and publishers of this book can in no way be held responsible if you get taken up on this offer.)

If you want to be offensive to a woman, wait until she is being all hysterical, mopey, inadequate, incompetent, and then inquire, gently:

'Time of the month, dear?'

– and see where that gets you.

Wanting To Be Silly

Say:

'I'm all ears …'

Wanting To Stop The Conversation

The whole purpose of this book has been to make conversation flow and sparkle. There are, however, occasions when you may feel the need to stop conversations dead in their tracks. There are a number of useful phrases that can be employed to bring this about.

Lord Reith, the formidable and somewhat crusty guiding force behind the BBC in its early days, would use the Scotticism:

'I hear ye ...'

Used in response to a remark he did not agree with or thought beneath him even to consider discussing, these three words had a deeply unsettling effect on the hearer. Even when addressed to Malcolm Muggeridge in a TV interview they brought about a fraction of a second's silence.

Perhaps more polite but equally effective are mystifying comments beginning:

'If God had meant us to ...'

For example, 'If God had meant us to fly, he wouldn't have invented the railways'; 'If God had meant us to go to the dry cleaners, he wouldn't have invented the Hoover'; 'If God had meant us to believe in Him, He wouldn't have invented the Bishop of Durham'; and so on.

We can learn most in this field, however, from the sayings of the hard of hearing. Deaf people, willy-nilly, have discovered the art of putting a spoke in conversations from which they have rudely been excluded. Or, could it be, that they would not have wanted to take part in them anyway? Perhaps we shall never know.

My maternal grandmother was a past mistress at this sort of thing. The important thing was that, initially, she appeared willing to take part in conversation with us. She was deaf but she sported an enormous and very prominent deaf-aid. Not a hearing trumpet, that would have been too affected, but a vast dish, somewhere about the size of Goonhilly Down or Jodrell Bank, which she had pinned on the front of her capacious bosom. This she would turn in the direction from which she supposed sound was coming. She would then turn up the volume until all sorts of howls and whines were emitted. After a while, Grandma would give up the attempt, turn off the machine and relapse into brooding silence.

Then she would use another technique. Seeing from our laughing faces that a joke had been cracked, she would ask, 'What did he say?'

Some innocent would then begin to bellow the joke slowly and very loudly all over again in the direction of Grandma:

'WELL, YOU SEE, THERE WAS THIS COMMERCIAL TRAVELLER …'

And so it would go on, very painfully:

'AND HE DISCOVERED HE HADN'T BROUGHT HIS PYJAMAS …'

Grandma would sit there, straining to hear this terrible tale while we all writhed in agony at having to endure it all over again.

'SO THE LANDLORD'S DAUGHTER HAD TO SHARE A …'

This all took a very long time. Finally the punchline would hove into view:

'NINE MONTHS LATER, THE COMMERCIAL TRAVELLER HAPPENED TO BE …'

Slightly bemused, Grandma would attend the end of the recital:

'AND IT WAS STILL THERE ON THE TOP OF THE WARDROBE!'

By this time we would have to be scraped off the ceiling in extremities of agony. With unerring timing, Grandma would then pause a second and ask, in a strained voice, 'A commercial what-did-he-say?'

Superb! But Grandma's finest moment came once when we were sitting round the tea-table, debating one of the great issues of the day, and, as usual, excluding the poor old thing from the conversation. Suddenly, she erupted with the inquiry:

'How's your telephone, Bill?'

It took us a moment or two to realize that not one of us was called 'Bill'. It slowly dawned that she had embarked on one of her pet theories, that she was being over-charged for her telephone calls (not that she ever made any.) From that day, in our family, the phrase 'How's your telephone, Bill?' was ritually employed whenever anybody wanted to change the subject. Or to bring a conversation to a juddering halt.

Someone else's deaf granny devised the equally efficacious:

'But wasn't he a Smith-Bosanquet?'

– which has a similarly emasculating effect on conversation.

I also recall with pleasure the brilliant response made by a hard of hearing old neighbour, coming out of church. My mother turned to her and, wishing to make polite conversation, remarked, 'That was a very good sermon wasn't it?' Came the reply:

> **'Yes, but I don't think I'd go there for my holidays again ...'**

I think, when it comes to the gift of the gab, we have a lot to learn from the hard of hearing.